THE ADVANCED SLEUTH INVESTOR

Access your brain's hidden info,
to take other people's money

AVNER MANDELMAN

Author's note:

The case studies and anecdotes depicted in this book, as well as the occasional dialogues and speeches put in the mouth of characters, are fictionalized narration (in the old tradition of Greek historians) inspired by folk tales told by persons engaged in business, politics, and the military, and should not be considered accurate or true representation of real historical, political, or commercial events. Such tales present both personages who succeeded and therefore may appear heroic, and those who had failed and therefore may seem inept or worse. Neither is wholly true. In no matter which arena of life they strive, all such human actors do what they can, and whether they succeed or not is often up to fate and luck. In that regards Teddy Roosevelt's "Man in the Arena" is an apt metaphor, serving to make clear that the author doesn't intend to offend any person, entity, or group of people. None of the book's contents should be seen as investment or legal advice and are to be viewed as educational material only. Readers are directed to consult their financial and legal advisers and do their own due diligence before acting on any ideas expressed in this book. Caveat lector.

 The author may be contacted at PO Box 26062, Toronto RPO Broadway, Ontario M4P 0A8, Canada

ISBN (paperback) 978-1-7388044-0-5
ISBN (e-book) 978-1-7388044-1-2
ISBN (hardcover) 978-1-7388044-2-9

Edited by Graham Southorn
Cover Design Indie Publishing Group Inc
Interior Design Indie Publishing Group Inc
Cover illustration by Shady Curi

To my former Gordon Capital partners, who changed Canada's finance.

OTHER BOOKS BY THE AUTHOR:

The Debba, 2010, Other Press / Random House, NYC, 2010
Le Testament de Jaffa, 2010, Editions Liana Levy, Paris, 2010
The Sleuth Investor, McGraw Hill, NYC, 2007
Talking to the Enemy, Seven Stories Press, NYC, 2006
Parlare al Nemico, Il Punto d'Incontro, Milan, 2006
Cuckoo, Oberon Press, Ottawa, 2003
Talking to the Enemy, Oberon Press, Ottawa, 1998.

CONTENTS

INTRODUCTION

A CONTRACT, A PLAN, AND A PRE-BATTLE REHEARSAL

A. CONTRACT WITH THE READER

Do you want to become a rich top investor?

This book will both show you how, and prove why sleuth investing is the best method to take you to the top.

My first book, *The Sleuth Investor*, revealed the basics of sleuth investing. In effect: how to dig for exclusive, physical information about individual stocks so as to take the money of those who prefer to stay home and "invest" only via Internet "information."

This book will go further.

Using advanced sleuth investing principles, it will both show you how to become a rich top investor with a *portfolio* of top-performing stocks, and prove to you *why* sleuth investing is the method that will take you to the top.

But before we start:

Let's make sure we are in agreement about what this book *will* do, what it *won't*; and who you the reader *are*. This should help me visualize you and speak to you directly—and help *you* understand what to expect. Once we agree, I'll state the urgent problem of yours I propose to solve and how I aim to solve it; I'll tell you what my qualifications are for this job, and finally I'll go ahead and do it.

That's the plan.

In a way, it's a contract between me, the author, and you the reader: A few hours of your time (and the book's price) in exchange for a solution to your problem, clearly explained.

So: Who am I addressing?

WHO ARE YOU, THE READER?

First and foremost, you are a well-educated, well-read, intelligent investor with a brokerage account. Not necessarily an expert, but one with a good education and some experience. You are probably working as a professional in an office, investing in your spare time. Or maybe you are an investment pro, an analyst, or even a money manager, perhaps with a CFA or an MBA degree or studying for one. Still, in your heart of hearts, you are also curious. Like the university student you once were, you care not only *how* things work but also *why* they do. That's also why, when you began to invest, you educated yourself about investing, certain that it would help you become rich.

And yet it doesn't seem to work.

You've read investment books, including my first one (I hope), Benjamin Graham's, Warren Buffett's letters and maybe even Philip Fisher's and Peter Lynch's, but you are more than just a market denizen. You have a university degree, perhaps even a few, and you've studied science or engineering or history or politics, or even several of the above. You've read Machiavelli and *Moby Dick*, and both *Alice in Wonderland* and *Through the Looking Glass*, from which you can quote Jabberwocky's opening lines, perhaps even all of it.

In short, you consider yourself sophisticated, broad-minded, and well-informed. That's who and what you are besides being an investor.

And now, before you continue reading, just so there's no misunderstanding:

WHAT THE BOOK WILL NOT DO FOR YOU:

If you're a trader, this book cannot help you become better at it. But if you are one, the book can at least show you how to avoid having your money taken by stock sleuths like me... And hopefully it can also convince you to become a sleuth yourself.

If you only read *Bloomberg* and *The Wall Street Journal*, this book cannot endow you with the wider book knowledge that top investors have: not only of investing, but also of science and literature and history, and (yes) philosophy of science. But if you'd like to see a sample of such books, you can find them in the further reading section.

Last but not least: this is not a "paint by numbers" book like a CFA manual (see glossary of terms), or Joel Greenblatt's *The Little Book That Beats the Market* (see the reference section), or even Graham and Dodd's stock-picking method. In other words, it is not a "How to," step-by-step manual. Of course, the book includes advanced sleuthing tricks (including one or two sifting formulas) but they are not just numbers-related. Besides, the "How to" methods are only half the story here. The other half is the "Why." That is, solid *proofs* of why this book's claims are true. The ratio of "How" to "Why" chapters is roughly 50/50.

Look, I am not trying to dissuade you from reading my book... I just want to set your expectations straight.

Now, you may ask:

Why do I need proofs? Why waste space that could be used for further case studies and "How to" techniques?

For two reasons.

CREDIBILITY, AND CONVICTION

First reason: Because this book's claims may appear to some readers hard to believe, especially the first claim that *some information cannot be named, i.e., encapsulated in math and language*—what I'll call Dark Information. The second claim is even harder to believe: that *your brain (and those of your market opponents) is blind to this unnamable Dark Info*. But the third and hardest claim to believe (for nearly all) is that if you know how, *you can find this unnamable Dark Info inside your own brain and access it*, so as to take the money of those who cannot do it.

The first two claims have been proven in several scientific disciplines (math, physics). But unless you are a mathematician or a physicist, they may sound so unlikely that if I don't prove them right up front, you'd be fully justified in not believing me. However, proof of the third claim is *very* recent. It is based on the latest findings of a top Neural Net scientist, which, coupled to long-established findings of how the brain's cortex works, can give you a great edge in the market, so long as you do the necessary work needed to make use of it.

The second reason I spend time on proving the above claims is that you'll need solid proofs to develop **a strong conviction** in the method. Just like in war, where soldiers fight hard only when they're convinced that what they're doing is right, so it is in investing. Unless you're absolutely convinced, you won't go all out to sleuth physically for what others are blind to. And if you won't do it, your money, just like traders' money, will be prey to sleuths like me, and it won't get you what you want.

BUT WHAT *DO* YOU WANT?

Put simply, you'd like to be rich because you deserve to afford the best of everything to which your top education and well-read mind have prepared you. Yet you see, all around you, even common folks with no education whatever getting rich through stocks. Surely, you ask yourself, how come they can and I cannot? You certainly know more than they do, and have more degrees and more education, which should help you become rich. And yet it doesn't.

Why doesn't it?

You probably know enough about investing by now (through your reading), to realize that *to make investing worth your while, you must outperform the market.* Else why bother? Because if you can't do better than the market, you should just buy the market's ETF, the SPY (see glossary of terms), then go to the beach and wait for your wealth to roll in, although a bit more slowly.

WHAT'S THE PROBLEM YOU WRESTLE WITH?

Yet despite all your scholarly degrees and diligent investing, *you still haven't managed to outperform the market.* And although (I hope) you've read my first book, *The Sleuth Investor* (*TSI*), you've found it bothersome to do what it recommends—perform physical investigations—so you've gone back to your old ways of Internet "investing."

Because, let's face it, the Internet has all the information you need, doesn't it? Especially for an educated professional like you, who knows how to handle information. (Else you wouldn't have gotten your degrees.) And the Internet certainly has enough info to use the Graham and Dodd / Warren Buffett method of "value investing by the numbers," which you have studied. So why doesn't it work for you, with all your qualifications?

After all, that's how the masters do it. Don't they? And *they* are beating the market.

Or are they?

Let me tell you a secret.

VALUE INVESTING STOPPED WORKING FOR THE MASTERS, TOO

For the last *fifteen years*, the vast majority of value investors, including the masters noted above, have *failed to outperform the market.* And this includes Buffett & Munger (barely), and Carl Icahn, and other celebrated value investors. And yes, it's true also for value ETFs. All have done worse than the market. Often much worse.

You don't believe me?

BERKSHIRE HATHAWAY HAS NOT OUTPERFORMED FOR 15 YEARS

Take the stock price of Buffett's company, BRK, A or B, and plot it over the last 15 years. Yes, it has gone up. But how did it do against the market?

To find that out, plot BRK/A divided by SPY, the S&P500 ETF, on any charting program. The SPY trades in huge volume and pays a dividend too, which BRK doesn't.

So: Does this ratio line go up, or down?

AN INDEX FUND WITH GREAT PR

If you include the SPY's dividends, reinvested over 15 years in the SPY (at zero commission), the ratio line is flat. (This is written in September 2022). Which means that over the last 15 years—half a generation—Warren and Charlie have been running an S&P500-equivalent index fund without a dividend—which the SPY does pay.

But yes, BRK has one advantage over the SPY: it has excellent PR.

Why do I say excellent?

Because despite its 15 years' market-matching performance, tens of thousands of wide-eyed acolytes still descend yearly on Omaha, Nebraska, in a wild capitalistic Woodstock, to listen to Warren and Charlie speaking from the dais. Even though over the last half-generation they have done no better than the general market.

Why have Warren and Charlie not done better?

PERHAPS IT'S THE PORTFOLIO SIZE

Is it because they run $950 billion in assets?

Yes, that's likely a part of it. With $950 billion in assets, even a $9.5 billion investment is a mere 1% addition to the portfolio.

Also, let's not forget, Buffett keeps a high portion of his portfolio in cash, which is not "working." But since Buffett is a phenomenal investor, genius-smart with an amazing work ethic, you might have thought that over 15 years he would still have outperformed the SPY.

But he hasn't.

Or are the portfolio size and the unused cash the *only* reason? Maybe it's also because Warren and Charlie leave their corporate holdings alone and don't try to "fix" them? Maybe it's the passivity?

That can't be it either. Just recently, it came to light that Buffett stood up to Coca-Cola's board, which tried to vest management stock options a bit too fast. And he did it both diplomatically (by abstaining) and effectively. (They sheepishly changed the vesting period.)

But the Coca-Cola affair was not what Buffett and Munger often do. They are "mere" choosers of stocks and choosers of price, not turnaround artists.

So maybe that's what creates market overperformance? Active "fixit" skills?

Nope.

To show this, let's look at Carl Icahn's company, Icahn Enterprises. (Stock symbol: IEP.)

IT'S NOT THE ACTIVE FIXING EITHER

Carl Icahn is the quintessential activist value investor. He buys companies for value, changes boards, fires ho-hum CEOs, sells unneeded divisions, and cuts costs. The stories he tells about it are wonderfully funny. Just look him up on YouTube, doing his schtick about how he and Leon Black of Apollo Partners tried to take over US Steel. Why, if Icahn ever retired, he could be a stand-up comic any time and sell tickets.

But what about his performance record?

Ah. Look at the chart of IEP:SPY— that's Icahn's public company compared to the SPY. Over the last 15 years, this ratio line has been sloping down.

Well, well. It seems that for the last half-generation, not only couldn't the granddaddy of passive value investing, Warren Buffett, outdo the market, but Carl Icahn, the daddy of value activists, couldn't outdo it either.

IS IT THE MEGA CAP OF THEIR INVESTMENTS?

Or perhaps Buffett and Icahn couldn't outdo the SPY because both invest in big behemoth companies? Maybe if they had invested in midcaps—which you can do—they'd do better?

Let's look then at the MidCap value ETF, IJJ, divide it by the SPY, and examine the chart. How did it do?

It looks even worse. Down, down.

WHAT OF INTERNATIONAL VALUE, THEN?

So (you now say a bit desperately), what if we look at *international* value? Not just North American stocks? Maybe value abroad is where outperformance resides?

Alright, look at the chart of IVAL, International Value ETF, divided by the SPY. How did it do?

Even worse.

Alright. So maybe value investors underperform because both passive and active value investing, whether at home or abroad, attempts to find value by *historical* numbers. What if we included earnings *forecasts*? Done by the best analysts?

FORECASTS DO NOT BRING OVERPERFORMANCE EITHER

Let's look then at the AllianceBernstein ETF, ABVAX. Bernstein's are, in my opinion, among the best analysts on Wall Street, not beholden to corporate finance. Years ago, when I ran research at BBN, Bay Street's (Canada's Wall Street) top research boutique, all my analysts (and me also) were voted No. 1 in their areas, and I used Bernstein as a benchmark for excellence.

So how did Bernstein's value fund do?

Look at the ratio line ABVAX:SPY. Worse and worse still.

But wait, you still say, maybe we are being *too* clever? Why not *just buy cheapness, and wait*?

NOR IS OUTPERFORMANCE DUE TO BACK-TESTING

Well, then. Let's look at Jim O'Shaughnessy, who back-tested cheapness strategies based on low Price/Sales, Price/Book, P/E, or what have you. He's been using Compustat's database of all companies' financial statements, as I often did, during my career as a money runner.

How did his back-tests do?

They look better—*in theory*. Just look up his splendid book, *What Works on Wall Street*. But if you try to do it in *real* time, it doesn't seem to work, as his funds based on his research have shown. His book's back-tested overperformance was likely due to phantom trades of small caps without much volume.

So, what's going on here?

How come none of the value masters could do better than the market over the last 15 years? Either passive, active, US or international, with or without analysts' forecasting input, or even with back-testing based on the company's financial statements?

A MERE 8% OUTPERFORM THE MARKET—AND NOT CONSISTENTLY EITHER

But what about *other* kinds of funds?

Say growth, not value? Or maybe a combo of the two? Or perhaps turnaround funds? Or EVA funds (yes, there are such). Or any other kinds of funds, run by the best minds in the business? How many of these outperform the plain old S&P500?

In a word, almost none.

Here is what Dow Jones & Co said in 2018: the percentage of active managers who do beat the market is less than 8%—and even these don't do it consistently, i.e., finding such sometime-heroes is a toss-up. So, for many investors, the ability to invest in index funds and outperform 92% of all fund managers seems like a no-brainer.

Why invest at all then, on your own?

Well, then.

Why compete in the Boston marathon, one of thousands of runners, when only three can win? Why spend years writing a novel, when only a few are published and fewer still win awards? Why practice the violin (or piano) three hours a day, aiming to be a concert performer, when only one or two in a hundred have a chance of making it?

WHY WORK HARD TO EXCEL?

In the same defeatist spirit, why aim to outperform the market on your own when you can just buy an index fund or a market ETF and outdo 92% of everyone else?

Come to think of it, why try to excel in *anything* when you can just sit at home, sip coffee, and watch Netflix? Why work hard, aiming to outdo 95%, or 98%, or even reach the very top?

The honest answer is:

Seeking excellence is not for everyone, yet some seek it because they refuse to be average. No matter how hard it is to excel.

Are you one of these?

If you picked up this book after reading my first one, you probably are.

INVESTING AS PERFORMANCE ART

Those who refuse to be average see investing as performance art. Just as Olympic athletes see their sport, or top-level violinists and pianists see music, or fiction writers see books, or stage magicians see magic, or top painters see their art.

You think this comparison is over the top?

Think again: Warren Buffett himself said of his investing, "It's my canvas." He, too, sees it as an art form, and so do I. And if this comparison strikes a chord in you, most likely so do you.

Therefore, when Dow Jones & Co. tells you to just buy the SPY, be average and go to the beach, you'd probably refuse, saying: *I* can do better.

And so you can.

But how can you, if even the masters lately could not?

THE SOLUTION IS SLEUTHING

You *can* do better than the market, maybe *much* better, if you sleuth companies properly, as per my first book. That is, on top of the *public* info, you dig for *physical* information that is *true, important,* and *exclusive* (to you), *before* it becomes ink or bits. And you can get such info *only* by sleuthing the companies behind the stocks *yourself,* and do it *physically,* not via the Internet.

But will you?

MOST LIKELY YOU WILL NOT

Sadly, as I said above, based on conversations with readers of my first book, probably not.

What many readers tell me is that they loved the book, understood the method, enjoyed the anecdotes, and yet have not done much sleuthing themselves.

Why not?

For two reasons, both of them from readers:

INCONVENIENCE, AND TOO MUCH EDUCATION

The first is inconvenience. It's inconvenient to leave home or the office to talk to strangers, so as to glean executives' true character, check physical facilities, or learn products' flaws via competitors, instead of sipping coffee restfully at your desk and going click-click / buy-sell on the Internet, with "free" info your only input.

However, second and more insidious, *most investors are way overeducated.* And this again applies to me also, and probably to many of you as well: engineers, computer experts, mathematicians, physicists, data scientists, lawyers, biotech PhDs, military historians…

But just why is overeducation a drawback?

INTELLECTUALS TAUGHT ALL INFO CAN BE STORED IN INK AND BITS

Because during your long university years, you were taught that *all information about anything can be represented as data,* which can be stored as print in documents (or books) or bits in computers, to be retrieved and manipulated, so as to forecast future events in the *real* world.

Therefore, once you began to invest, *you automatically assumed that investing too, was a science of manipulating stored data.* The kind you get on the Internet, mostly for free, *gathered by others.* You only have to learn how to *manipulate* it. Right?

WRONG: IT ISN'T TRUE

In my first book, I showed you why *this is false,* then showed you how to take the money of those who believe it *is* true—by doing *original* sleuthing work, to get *physical* information that your market opponents do not have.

Many readers responded enthusiastically and told me how much it helped their market gains. I still get emails.

But not all readers.

I found that quite a few readers, especially the highly educated ones, didn't *really* believe there's information *outside* stored data. After all, they use stored data for their jobs daily. Don't they?

Don't you?

Which is why, even though they'd enjoyed my first book and the case studies, the overeducated readers kept going click-click / buy-sell at their desks. Which meant they kept viewing the full-color, 3-D stock-market battles through a 2-D, black-and-white filter, while still expecting to win and outperform…

Which of course they haven't.

And if you, too, have likewise remained chained to your desk and the Internet, so haven't you.

Hence this book.

B. THE BOOK'S PLAN

WHAT I PROPOSE TO DO:

As said at the beginning, this book intends to *prove* to you that data stored in ink and bits (like financial statements, or corporate filings, or price charts) is not the *only* kind of data possible. There's also *another* kind of data, *raw, physical, uncategorizable data*, both about people and things, stored in *another* part of your brain, a part that makes decisions *differently*. Without math or calculations.

And why does this matter?

Because if you can access the *other* data in that *other* part of your brain, you can take the money of those overeducated intellectuals who rely only on *stored* data.

And then market overperformance—and wealth—are yours for the taking.

USING YOUR HIDDEN BRAIN

But just before you roll your eyes and throw away the book...

The above is not some new-age mumbo jumbo. It is based on the Nobel-prize winning work of Kahneman and Tversky, as summarized in Kahneman's seminal book, *Thinking Fast and Slow* (aka "System 1" and "System 2" thinking). As well, neuroscientist Jeff Hawkins hints at this in his two great books, *On Intelligence* and *A Thousand Brains*. He shows that the brain is an ongoing forecaster—but *only on categorized data, pre-processed* by the cortex from the chaotic inflow of sensory information, because categorized data is the *only* kind that allows orderly, scientific, "System 2" thinking. For example, science, math, or "CFA-type" analysis of financial statements. Yes, the kind that underperforms the market...

Now, what about "System 1" thinking?

Good question.

In his groundbreaking research into Neural Networks, Prof Naftali Tishby of Hebrew University found that during the categorizing process of raw inputs, *data that cannot be categorized are purposefully discarded.*

Or, as he puts it, *forgetting is an essential part of learning* (aka "generalization"). Which is what your brain does, to use "System 2" thinking (and then underperform).

THE WORLD AND ITS NAMES ARE NOT THE SAME THING

But just how does this "forgetting" relate to investing?

It relates to it directly, because Tishby's rule applies not just to Neural Nets, but also to the brain. And as Jeff Hawkins' work indicates, your brain too uses a Neural Net in the cortex's six layers (called Vernon Mountcastle's algorithm), to pre-processes your chaotic sensory data into *categories,* to which it gives *names.* Like letters, or numbers, or lengths, or "Assets," or "Liabilities," or "Profit." And only on these *names* can your brain do "System 2" thinking. That is, not on the *physical* information itself, but on its categorized *names.* That's how the brain does science, or math, and, yes, CFA-type investing, or, indeed, all "Intellectual work."

Yes, the kind you got your degree(s) for.

So once again: Just why does this matter to you, as an *investor*?

"NAME IT AND TAME IT." BUT WHAT OF THE UNTAMED REMAINDER?

Because while CFAs' brains do fancy "System 2" thinking on the company's financials (hence the name Chartered *Financial* Analyst), the *discarded* / uncategorizable info is not completely gone, and is available for doing "System 1" thinking, too.

But available where?

Why, it's stored in *another* part of your brain, the kind that does instinctive, "System 1" thinking—and *that* info is what we sleuths are after.

That's where our edge is—and it can also be yours.

INVESTING IS NOT SCIENCE, BECAUSE ITS AIMS ARE DIFFERENT

Ironically, Kahneman and Tversky's work was mostly about how to *avoid* "instinctive" "System 1" decision-making. Because, as they found, "System

1" is only 70-80% correct. Therefore, their work aims to make you slow down to methodical, scientific "System 2" thinking, which, though slower, is more accurate.

However, such accuracy is *true only for science, not for investing*, since **science and investing are *not* the same**—although if you are one of the overeducated, you probably *think* they are. But of course, they are not.

Science is a *philanthropic, public* activity, dedicated to finding the Rules of the World, then telling all humanity about them (in papers with copious footnotes) for free, so that *everyone* can be better off. Kumbaya.

Investing, however, is just the *opposite*. It is a *selfish* and *secretive* activity. It's about finding out the Rules of the Market, then *keeping them to yourself* and taking everyone *else's* money, so that only you (and your loved ones) are better off.

Therefore, the question now becomes:

How can you access the hidden area in your brain with the *uncategorized* data? The data discarded by your cortex after it has kept only the categories on which CFAs can do "System 2" thinking?

In other words, how to do what CFAs and other intellectual investors *cannot*, and *do not* do?

LOAD YOUR HIDDEN BRAIN WITH PHYSICAL FACTS

The way to do it is to load your hidden brain with *physical, exclusive* facts about the company, its people, product, customers, and environment—but facts that *you* unearth and generate *yourself*. Not public facts copied out of databases, or off the Internet. The sleuthed facts must be the fruit of *your* work, not of others.

Why is that?

For two reasons: first, obviously, for the exclusivity. But second, for the *emotional connection*, because it is the latter that activates "System 1" thinking.

As you'll see in the coming cases, only if the facts are due to *your* work will they be personal and emotional *for you*, and so stored in that *other* part of *your* brain. And when this info then comes up, your instinct uses the attached emotions to coat it with *the correct level of conviction*, that *you*—and nobody else—developed during the sleuthing.

Such info would "only" be 70-80% right, as Kahneman and Tversky found. Lower than what logical "System 2" gets, *in matters of science.* However, as shown above, investment *isn't* science, though it often uses its methods. And besides, 70-80% correct isn't bad, is it?

However, what about the wrong 20%-30% of "System 1" decisions?

Well, there you use money management rules, risk-control techniques, and other basics of investing which you must *practice daily*, using methods employed by other winners in many other disciplines: the military, the arts, sports, and yes, science.

Practice how?

C. REHEARSALS FOR TOP PERFORMERS, BEFORE SHOWTIME

High-level professionals practice the basics regularly, *before* they perform on stage, so as to correct their mistakes in advance. Violinists play scales and practice techniques daily, as do pianists, as do Olympic athletes, top gymnasts, stage magicians, ballet dancers, and, yes, high-level commando soldiers before operations. Well before, so as to minimize errors during combat.

Have you ever practiced investing?

I'd bet that you haven't even heard about practicing basic investment techniques in a safe environment, before you've invested a single, real dollar.

And no, I don't mean picking stocks. That part is what everyone fixes on. Not that it's easy, but in my estimation, it's only 30-40% of the art. The rest is the ongoing buying and selling (and *holding*) of stocks in a portfolio, as the market storms around you and you must decide whether to act, and if so where and how much, or not to act, and if so, for how long. This performing art of portfolio management is the closest thing I know to real war (yes, I've fought in one), or to boxing several rounds against a hard, wily opponent. (Ditto.)

This practicing of the investing arts under real conditions, before you go live with your hard-earned money, will be the book's last chapter, where you'll learn how to put it all together.

But first and foremost, you must teach yourself to use your "hidden brain," so as to get the hidden information that most other investors are oblivious to.

HOW TO CONVINCE YOU OF ALL THIS?

To do this, I must first convince you that it is indeed necessary: That there *is* information that *cannot* be categorized, contra whatever you've learned in classical (though not modern) science.

But how can I *prove* this to you so definitively that you feel compelled to leave your office, put on your gumshoes, and go sleuthing, so as to take the money of those who don't?

THE ANSWER: THE BERLITZ METHOD

If you learned a foreign language in high school, you most probably learned its grammar, a list of verbs, both regular and irregular, and a slew of rules of conjugation. You probably wrote an essay or two, perhaps even took dictation, to learn how to write and read the language.

Yes, that's one way, in which your logical brain (i.e., the cortex) is given explicit rules. But taught that way, you'll likely never learn to *speak* the language fluently and instinctively.

The far-better way to learn is the one popularized by the Berlitz school: *Do it first in safe surroundings*. The teacher begins to speak to you in the foreign language, occasionally explaining a word or two, trusting that you'll eventually "catch on" and figure out all the rules that are *implicit* in the language. And once you do, you find yourself speaking.

The part that "catches on" is a *different* part of your brain, the older part, which figures things out before they've been made into categories, or numbers, or rules by the evolved cortex.

That older brain is the part that sleuths use.

THE CASE METHOD

So, as in my first book, I'll present you with live cases of how your pre-intellectual brain can be used in sleuthing, then let you (or, rather, it) figure out how it's done. (These case methods, by the way, will also be part of the How. That is: an indirect instruction, but instruction nevertheless.) But since intellectual readers like you come from many disciplines, I'll outline cases from several such fields' point of view. Like accounting, physics, math, the military, history, law, and a few others—all of which have some attributes analogous to investing.

SEEING SLEUTHING FROM DIFFERENT VIEWPOINTS

As a result, this book is arranged in chapters that see sleuthing from different disciplines' viewpoints. You can read only the ones closest to your discipline, whatever that is, but hopefully, you'll read them all in order and soon see that the principle of "hidden data" applies to all.

Then, while intellectual CFAs (who haven't read the book) invest "by the numbers," and underperform, *you'll* invest by what the numbers *cannot* contain, after loading your brain in a certain way with *physical* data, which will awaken your brain's *other* part, the one that sleuths.

PAYOFF: THE DARK INFORMATION

The hidden information that cannot be expressed in words or numbers, we will call Dark Info. At first blush, you might think it's the equivalent of Harry Potter's nemesis, Lord Voldemort—"he who must not (or shall not) be named." But that's not true in our case. Harry Potter's dark villain must not be named, but he *can* be—in fact, we just did it—while the info *we* are after really *cannot* be named by definition. It is unnamable because *it has no categories, no contours*, and so is dark and invisible to your modern brain (the cortex). That said, it does exist in its original, unstructured form in some of the ancient parts of your brain. Only once you grasp what Dark Info is, can you fully realize how important it is, and then get sleuthing to generate it, as the next few case studies will demonstrate. And once you can do that, the world is your oyster.

No, not the world's *name*, but the world *itself*, in all its 3-D, colorful physical splendor. To plunge into and savor and enjoy with your newly found wealth.

MY QUALIFICATIONS: ABOVE AVERAGE WHERE IT COUNTS

Now, what qualifications do I have to make you these promises?

First, I have a BSc degree in Aeronautical Engineering (yes, Rocket Science), so my math grade is above average, and so is my physics grade. I worked both in France and in Canada designing planes, and also at a

Canadian particle accelerator during its design phase (where my physics got polished). Then I got a Stanford MBA and strayed to business and investments, where I used both applied math and physics in the market, analyzing Techs, until I found sleuth investing. And yes, I've used Neural Nets since their early days—enough to know what they can and cannot do— then ran teams of top-ranked analysts both in brokerage firms (one of which I turned around) and in hedge funds, two of which I co-founded. I also co-founded a Robo-adviser which was later sold to a financial behemoth, and am now semi-retired. (Semi because I still invest, and lecture in university, and mentor.) And yes, I also wrote a few books on the way. (Look them up.)

AND NOW, A CAVEAT:

This is *not* a book of science (hence: no footnotes). Scientific topics appear here only by way of *analogies* to the topic of investing. The same goes for the non-science disciplines, like history, or military intelligence. Besides proving the method is correct, my purpose is to convince you that no matter your original education, or overeducation, you'd better get out and sleuth (for which you'll find extra tools here), because if you don't, sleuths like me will take your money.

My methods are metaphor, analogy, and conjecture. If you are a scientist, and the latter points you in new directions, well and good. Just cite this book and give it credit. But remember that this is not my aim. Science aims to enrich humanity. My book aims to enrich *you*.

BUT WHY REVEAL ALL THIS? AM I NOT AFRAID OF ARMING MY MARKET OPPONENTS?

Inevitably, the same question that arose among readers of my first book (*TSI*), must arise now:

Am I not afraid that, once investors follow this book's instructions, *everyone* will become an experienced sleuth and so will render it more difficult for me to make money in the market by sleuthing?

The answer is a double no.

First, just as I said in TSI, many readers will still find it inconvenient to turn off the Internet and go do physical sleuthing. Also, some will find it doubly difficult to *practice* investing (as this book recommends), before they go fight it out with Mr. Market (and me) for real.

EVERY SLEUTH INVESTOR'S VIEW IS DIFFERENT—BUT STILL VALID

But second, as per Niels Bohr's and Einstein's view (noted later in the book), every observer's view, though different, is equally valid, *and so is every sleuth investor's view valid.* Public info that CFAs use is incomplete, just as classical physics' view is incomplete. Each sleuth adds to the public info by creating private-new-info in the category of his or her choice, so each sleuth can (in theory) outperform the market, in his or her own way. As can you.

But what if *everyone* became a sleuth? Can everyone outperform?

LAKE WOBEGON MARKET

That's an interesting question, bringing up shades of Lake Wobegon, that fictional town from a popular American radio program, where *everyone* is above average. But it is likely irrelevant. There will always be lazy investors who do not want to turn off the Internet, leave the house, and go sleuth for physical info. Their money is fair game. Just as mine and yours is, by the way.

Can all of us outperform? Certainly not all.

Can you?

Up to now you haven't. How can you correct that?

Read on. You may be pleasantly surprised.

ACKNOWLEDGEMENTS AND THANKS

My sincere gratitude to those who've read the book's draft or parts of it, and provided useful comments, my multi-degreed editor, Graham Southorn, Ruth Southorn (multi-degreed as well), Benjamin Friedlander of USCSC, professor emeritus and math expert (and a chess maven too), finance professor (and another GSB grad) Adeel Mahmood of McMaster University, whose students gave me their critique freely, Doug Hofstadter, professor of cognitive science and comparative lit at Indiana U, whose book (together with Emmanuel Sander) *Surfaces and Essences (*about the key role of analogies in human thinking) has nudged me to write this book. Thanks also to the several highly educated, multi-degreed market mavens of both Bay and Wall Streets and their European equivalents, who read the final draft and gave me their frank views, especially Eddie Palmgren and Niklas Savas of Redeye's *By the Book* podcast. Ditto for Amir Efrati of Brosh Capital, Julien Nono, Tom Stanley, and, of course, thanks to Marjorie Nicolaou, whose common sense is most uncommon, to Chrissy Hobbs and the team at Indie Publishing Group Inc, whose talents and zeal helped bring this book to life, as well as Adrian Stein, Jacob Stein, and Charles Williams, for their critique, error-catching zeal, and general moral support. If however there are still errors, mis-analogies or mis-conjectures remaining, the faults are mine and mine alone.

But enough for now.

Let's dive in, first into the data that your opponents, intellectual investors, and CFAs are going by: The company's Financial Statements—the ultimate categorized investment data.

What are the financial statements missing?

CHAPTER 1

ACCOUNTANTS' POINT OF VIEW

What Pacioli's accounting missed, but Machiavelli's "Prince" didn't.

About five hundred years ago, in the midst of the Renaissance, an Italian monk by the name of Luca Pacioli invented accounting.

Pacioli was a mathematician, a chess player, a bon-vivant, and Leonardo da Vinci's long-term boyfriend. He was probably also a genius of Leonardo's caliber, but with an arguably even bigger impact on human civilization—perhaps *much* bigger.

Unlike most monks who were educated in Latin, Pacioli was lucky to be educated in the vulgate, the common language, so he wrote his book, *Summa de Arithmetica*, in the common tongue also, and consequently, it could be read by anyone. And well read it indeed was: mainly by merchants, because the knowledge in it helped them get rich, but also by statesmen, because it helped them keep the state prosperous, and so stay in power.

Just how did Pacioli's book manage to do that?

Besides giving a few solutions to chess puzzles, and a bit of geometry instruction to schoolboys, Pacioli's book—for the first time ever—gave instruction in the Venetian method of bookkeeping and accounting—the one with debits and credits—which is used to this day.

A CAPITAL-FLOWS INSTRUMENT PANEL WITH THREE DISPLAYS

Pacioli treated capital as if it was "money energy" that could be accumulated, grown, or transferred, yet always moved in well-defined *categories* that could be measured and recorded. And most important: if capital went out of one category, it went into another.

Money-conservation physics, if you will.

With standard formats and twinned movements, the accounting method soon became an indispensable instrument panel for commercial operations, with three displays on it: (1) The balance sheet, (2) the cash flow statement, and (3) the income statement.

(The order here, by the way, is in its importance to sleuths. In many parts of the world, where CFAs rule, it is often different.)

The balance sheet showed the current state of the capital at a certain date; **the cash flow statement** showed the raw changes to it during a certain period; and **the income statement** showed the smoothed approximation of such changes.

There was also **a ledger** that served as a checkup for the displays' accuracy, but it was only a side panel, used for verification only.

The above three panels are what Warren Buffett, Ben Graham, Carl Icahn, indeed all value investors, go by.

And often it is their *only* data.

TWO KINDS OF BASIC CATEGORIES: STATIC, AND DYNAMIC

Pacioli's accounting categories came in two kinds: static, and dynamic. The static ones were assets and liabilities, showing how rich the owner was, and the dynamic ones—revenues and costs—showed changes in the static categories, i.e., the rise and fall in wealth.

Each of these major categories was further divided into finer categories. Like short- and long-term assets, and short- and long-term liabilities;

and various kinds of revenues and costs. Finally, there were still-finer categories of each of the latter, as well as named differences between them, like Working Capital (Current Assets less Current Liabilities), Shareholders' Equity (Total Assets less Total Liabilities), and so on.

CATEGORIES A HUGE ADVANCE

The mere fact that accounting divided money and capital into *categories* and these into *subcategories* was a huge advance. First, it made it easier to comprehend (the brain's left hemisphere assimilates data hierarchically), and second, it made accounting comparable to physics, another then-budding science that dealt with categories, like mass, speed, pressure, or energy, all of which could be computed and often transmuted into each other.

In other words, *accounting tried to make commerce into science*, using science's methods. In this it succeeded tremendously—but in reflecting commerce strictly in the mirror of numbers and categories, it also missed a lot.

Quite a lot, actually. And in that miss lies sleuths' golden opportunity. We'll get to that.

Back to accounting's beginning.

ACCOUNTING AS MONEY-PHYSICS

Just like in the emerging science of those early Renaissance days, where energy increased in one place only to be reduced in another, Pacioli's tracked-capital also moved in mirrored actions. A debit here was always joined by an equal credit (or negative debit) there. For example, Accounts Receivable (a short-term asset) being paid meant a debit in Accounts Receivable, with a corresponding credit in Cash (also a short-term asset). That is: you were now owed less, but had more cash. Similarly, a payment to a supplier meant a credit to Accounts Payable (a short-term liability) and a debit to Cash. That is, you now had less cash (an asset), but also owed less (a liability). And so on.

Commerce, in other words, advanced in discrete joint-steps, where two consenting parties acted in tandem, each acting to its own benefit, of its own free will, always maintaining balance. This by itself was an insight of genius. But there were other points of genius in the new method:

DIVISION OF HUMANITY INTO PRINCIPALS AND AGENTS

First was the way accounting (implicitly) divided users into principals and agents—although Pacioli did not call them that. He called them owners, those who took the risk of losing everything but could also profit wildly if those risks came through; and Employees and Suppliers, the owner's agents who, if they fulfilled the owner's instructions, were paid exactly what they were promised or owed, yet could win no more than that.

Clients, by the way, could be seen as agents also—they were suppliers of purchase orders and of cash. Now, mind: they could also be principals of their *own* operations, where they'd use what they had bought as raw material for their *own* enrichment. Of course, whether they did get rich or not depended entirely on their own will and talent.

TO EACH BASED ON HIS ABILITY, FROM EACH ACCORDING TO HIS NEED

In short, *accounting was a way of re-ordering the world* in such a way that each participant gained a profit (or was paid) based on his ability, and worked according to his need.

Three hundred years later, Karl Marx (whose un-peopled view of history was similar to Pacioli's view of commerce), inverted the order, with tragic consequences. We'll get to that in the next chapter, comparing stock analysis to historical analysis, with several useful lessons for your future sleuthing.

But back to Pacioli's accounting:

A NEW WORLD VIEW, AND UN-CHURCHY WORLD ORDER

Pacioli's unique division of humanity into principals and agents was a totally new thing. The old churchy view was that God was the only principal, with everyone else His (and the Holy Spirit's) agent. The Pope too, was a mere agent, and so were the Cardinals. Yes, kings were temporary principals, a role they could bequeath to their progeny, but unlike modern democracy (still 250 years away) where principals / rulers needed the consent of their governed / agents, kings made sure it was explicitly noted that *they* ruled By the Grace of God. That is, they were humble agents also, approved by the church, which was collectively an agent of His will also.

Thus, until accounting came along, everyone had to adhere to church law, and (at least on the surface) always appear to be moral and good, and do unto others as one wanted done unto him or her, because one had no choice but to serve others, always.

THE GOLDEN RULE STILL APPLIED—BUT SELFISHLY

Accounting, it should be noted, still adhered to that last part, aka the Golden Rule. A debtor expected to be paid by the borrower, just as he himself endeavored to pay his debt. But that was not a question of biblical diktat, but rather a question of utility: if one didn't pay, next time nobody would want to lend to one again.

Or, as the old Bible aptly said: A good name is better than good oil.

And so, contrary to biblical morality where one had to do as the Principal Above told one, or else, commercial morality, as expressed in Pacioli's accounting, was merely the preservation of one's credit rating out of self-interest. And all this was done through the new commercial science of accounting via its three instrument panels which served the owner / principal as a tool for realizing *his* vision. It also enabled him to do it efficiently and effectively, by allocating work to those who could do it cheapest and best—*which the instrument panel, for the first time, now let him measure with precision.*

The new accounting, in other words, *allowed owners to maximize their return on capital,* and so allowed humanity as a whole to grow fast, and so spread prosperity both among principals and among agents. Not according to some vague theory of churchy justice, but based on measured individual contributions done with mutual consent, and acceptance of risk according to one's appetite and intelligence.

Reminds you of the stock market? Wait. We'll get to it too.

A WEALTH-CREATING INSTRUMENT PANEL

As it took root, this new accounting science with its three scales—balance sheet, income statement, and cash flow statement— proved to be a miracle of wealth creation. If the merchant / owner minded his business properly—and his accounting books—he could get rich by ensuring he always sold above cost—which, before, he'd tried to do approximately, but now had a precise way of measuring, by tracking both sales and expenses.

But wait. How was profit calculated, exactly?

After all, a growing mercantile operation had to deal with many products, and so it had a variety of costs, as well as a variety of sales. Just imagine if you, as a budding stock sleuth, wanted to delve deep into such a company's operations. How could you determine whether all product sales were profitable, or whether some were not? And if so, which?

In other words, in a multi-product company, what is profit, what is loss?

So, yet again: How to compute profit?

"MATCHING": ACCOUNTING'S FIRST RULE

Hence, Pacioli's first rule of accounting was that of *matching*: Profit was sales less all expenses—highlight *all*—that gave rise to those sales.

Yet how to track "gave rise to?" In other words, the question of *matching* became intricately tied to the problem of *causation*. How could one know what caused sales? Or, as the old Latinists used to say, *Post hoc non est procter hoc*. Just because it follows, doesn't mean it's caused.

Thankfully, some parts of this causation problem were easy, but others were less so, and others still, very hard indeed. Because, it so transpired, sales had both *direct* costs (such as the cost of sand in the making of bricks), and *indirect* costs (such as the cost of the kiln), but also vague *background* costs, such as management salaries, none of which was directly attributable to any specific sales. And some costs were entirely uncertain, such as the occasional storm, or a war, that had to be borne but were not the cause of any sales (unless the merchant was in the insurance business or in arms sales).

COST ACCOUNTING IS BORN

This problem of *attribution*—what causes what, and how precisely—was one that would plague the profession of accounting for many years. Eventually, it manifested itself as cost accounting, where the key question was: Which products make money, which don't?

Those merchants who solved it successfully—for example, Wedgwood tableware in Britain—laid the foundation for a big fortune. And as an aside: Wedgwood Sr., for example, was Charles Darwin's grandpa, which meant that Darwin could have the leisure to pursue his Theory of Evolution by gallivanting around the globe. Thus, in a roundabout way, Pacioli's invention did help science, substantiating our prior claim that it helped Western civilization perhaps even more than Leonardo da Vinci (Pacioli's roommate) did.

ATTRIBUTION A RECURRING PROBLEM

However, normally such attribution of cause and effect is much more difficult, not just in history and in cost accounting. It also appears (much later) in management theory, which asks which action of a company's leader contributed to success, and which leader's action simply piggy-backed on the company's existing advantages (which will be seen later as akin to the primal question of historians). And if so, how to attribute each causal factor to eventual success, and in what amount, so as to know (1) what to do more of, (2) do by whom, and (3) how to pay those doers properly.

And just to push the point of similarity and reappearance of key questions:

The question of attribution would also reappear later in other sciences of results maximization, such as the working of Neural Networks, the working of your brain, or, yes, the mechanisms (if any) of stock forecasting.

But let's not jump too far ahead. Back again to the Renaissance.

Clearly, Pacioli's invention was a marvel, with obvious advantages to both merchants and rulers. But what were its shortcomings? For surely it had some too?

ACCOUNTING'S SHORTCOMINGS

Yes it did, and many such, most due to the fact that *in the three instrument panels, no people appeared.* None. People, as in humans, those highly evolved chimps whose actions and talents cannot always be categorized or quantified, let alone be attributable to causes, or shown to *be* causes. (We'll see this too, later, in the chapter about Turing's Test.)

In plain words: top management, middle management, the company's directors, employees, suppliers, clients, family alliances or strife, common (or disparate) social backgrounds or unifying beliefs of the above, were manifest only implicitly, in the money-numbers that these people produced—or consumed, either collectively, or individually. For, without easy attribution, who could tell who did what, specifically, and who merely helped, or hindered, and by just how much?

ACCOUNTING'S IGNORANCE OF PEOPLE A CLEAR DEFICIENCY

One couldn't. Because, in Pacioli's three instrument panels, any specific person filling a function, say CEO, or CFO, or CIO, was just like any other. Same as in the game of chess (which will have an analogy-chapter of its own) where all kings are the same, as are all queens, all knights, and all pawns. Similarly, from the point of view of a CFA, who only analyzes a company's financial statements, it is immaterial whether the CEO is a Steve Jobs, a Bill Gates, a Warren Buffett, a Meg Whitman, a Mary Barra, or, to take the other side, an IBM former CEO (who'll stay unnamed). The only impact would be circuitous, via the numbers the CEO had produced (maybe)—or consumed, or (again maybe), perhaps helped destroy (maybe, maybe).

Or perhaps not?

Perhaps the company was in such a bad way that no one could help it? How to know?

AND SO IS CFA'S AND VALUE INVESTING'S PEOPLE-IGNORANCE

On this, Pacioli's accounting said little. Yes, it did give some help (credit rating and risk came into it), but not nearly enough. Certainly not enough to forecast both success and failure, except in extreme cases, and even then, not always.

Just as in Graham and Dodd's value investing, and Greenblatt's magic formula, and CFA manuals 1 to 3, only numbers matter. Only numbers. People are fungible.

But are they?

They aren't, of course. And it is this very lack of non-numerical information in accounting that gives us sleuths an opening (one of them), because not only people are missing in Pacioli's financial scales, but other things too. Many other things. Big ones.

For example: accounting only deals with distinct *categories* of commerce, those that can be quantified, and parsed.

But are these the only ones possible? Are there perhaps *other* commercial factors that can neither be categorized nor quantified, yet are important?

Oddly enough, this very question dogs many other fields analogous to investing, including modern science, for example quantum physics, where non-categories, perhaps even non-categorizable, show as extremely important.

But all in good time. We'll get to that too.

MACHIAVELLI'S BOOK DID WHAT PACIOLI'S DID NOT

Niccolo Machiavelli, who lived not far from Pacioli and at about the same time, did not make the same mistake of disregarding the importance of exceptional people. In his own book, *Il Principe*, he answered the first question of history, which we'll meet in the next chapter (Who makes whom? History or leaders?) in a way just as extreme as Pacioli's—but totally opposite:

Whereas Pacioli implied that only numbers mattered, Machiavelli implied that only people did. And exceptional people at that, for whom non-churchy behavior was, paradoxically, often the ultimate morality.

And yes, Machiavelli's rulers could use accounting also, but not just to gain wealth. Contrary to Pacioli's book, where the aim of owners' power was to gain wealth, period, the aim of Machiavelli's Principals was to use wealth (inter alia) so as to gain power and keep it, but with the ultimate aim of attaining glory and fame, and so enter into history.

Machiavelli, by the way, was educated in high-class Latin and worked as a diplomat for several rulers, and so perhaps not incidentally, unlike Pacioli, he wrote his book not for everyone but for rulers, for whom he worked, to help them obtain power over other agents such as himself.

And yes, he too wrote his book in Italian, though not the vulgate, as Pacioli had, but the formal language. (However, the headings of the chapters were in Latin.)

Yet there were two other differences between Pacioli's *Summa* and *Il Principe*. Major ones.

PACIOLI WROTE WHAT OUGHT TO BE, MACHIAVELLI WHAT IS

The first difference: Pacioli's *Summa's* accounting taught dispassionately how things ought to be, always, for everyone, principals/owners and agents/employees and customers and suppliers alike. Everyone ought to keep his or her word, for example in the matter of debt, both because of the law, and because otherwise one would lose one's credit and be unable to obtain a loan again.

Machiavelli's *Il Principe*, per contra, was the direct opposite—because it was *not* for everyone. It recommended that the ruler keep his word *only* when it was advantageous to him, and break it when it was necessary—because there was no law above staying in power.

In other words, Machiavelli's book was *not* about how things ought to be, but rather of how things really, truly were, X-rated and R-rated and unspeakable, which you, O ruler, ought to know of, or you will not last. But just do it. Never talk about it.

Which, in a way, is also what my book, modesty aside, tries to tell you. But we'll get to that too.

THE X-RATED TRUTH SHALL SET YOU FREE. BUT DO KEEP YOUR MOUTH SHUT ABOUT IT

As a sleuth investor, you too must know what companies and stocks really and truly are—that is, unlike their G-rated, clean and tidy financial statements. Most of this truth you can find out only by yourself, because no one, but really no one, will tell it to you. Neither newspapers (pressured by politicians and advertisers), nor Wall Street (which claims to be your financial servant), and certainly not government, because *its* problems of staying in power are top of its mind, not yours.

And yes, all the above have read *Il Principe* and follow its advice, especially the best-known one: that *the good servant will always be a servant*, which is both an incitement and advice in one.

A minor side-bar is due here:

Although Machiavelli did not use the words principal and agent either—certainly not in the sense they are used today, yet his book, *Il Principe*, carried half of this word-pair in its title. That book's title is commonly translated as *The Prince*, but should more properly be translated as *The Principal*: he who rules over his subjects.

And just to make sure we're all on the same page, here is the standard definition of both A and P:

An agent is a person who gets paid to realize someone else's vision, in exchange for money, a bonus, a medal, and life-meaning. The great majority of people are agents.

A principal is a person who pays agents (with the above) to realize his. Principals are very few.

Both types are necessary in all human groupings, whether civilian, military or commercial.

Now, just to make clear:

Being agent or principal says nothing about a person's goodness or badness. For example, Napoleon was a principal whose vision was being Emperor, even at the price of misery and death to many others. He was clearly bad. Wellington and Nelson were agents who toppled him and liberated Europe (sort of). They were, compared to Napoleon, good.

And there are, of course, opposite cases of bad and good, in all possible combinations.

Whether principals are born or raised is a hard problem, and is related to history's prime question, so let's defer it to Chapter 3, where its relevance to sleuthing will be made clear.

Machiavelli certainly didn't miss the importance of top people (principals), as his book's name proves. So, while Pacioli wrote his book for commercial principals, that is, owners, who pay agents to realize their (the owners') vision of wealth, Machiavelli wrote his book for political principals, whose vision was not wealth but power, which the ruled had to help their principal realize, in exchange for other emoluments.

COMMERCIAL AGENTS AND POLITICAL ONES ARE PAID DIFFERENTLY

As for the last:

Pacioli's employees were paid in cash by the owner/principal, and customers were paid in products and/or services. Everything was coldly commercial.

Machiavelli's agents/subjects, on the other hand, were paid differently by the ruler/principal. Although in one respect they were more like customers, since they paid the ruler in taxes, and in the occasional military service. Yet the "product" they received in exchange was not just the rule of law, within which *they* could become commercial principals and get rich, like Pacioli's crass merchants, but they also received titles and ranks and civic pride and life-meaning, which, in many cases, were as important to them as the rest, sometimes more.

CIVIC PRIDE EXISTS IN SOME COMPANIES, TOO

Now why do I mention these here?

Because these latter benefits are worthy things to sleuth for, when you query corporate informers. Companies that manage to pay with pride and a sense of purpose often create additional shareholders' value, which is uncategorizable and therefore unseen by CFA types. It's one more advantage that sleuths have. We'll get to that in a few later cases involving sleuthing techniques.

But before we leave the topic of wealth: Just what does *getting rich* mean?

Yes, of course, it means *owning more*. But what does *owning* mean?

WHAT IS OWNERSHIP, EXACTLY?

That question is far more important than you might think. And to answer it, we must re-examine the balance sheet, where ownership appears.

The balance sheet is a double-exposure snapshot of the company at a point in time. It is taken by the company's official financial photographer (aka the auditor) once a quarter or year for financial reporting, or once a month (by the CFO, or the controller) for operational reporting.

REAL LEFT AND FICTIONAL RIGHT

That snapshot has two lists displayed side by side. The left side is (mostly) a real (physical) list, while the right side is mostly a (non-physical) fictional list.

In other words: The left side contains mainly real things, like machinery, buildings, cash, and invoices, and the right side mostly *names* of things, or even names of names. Like mortgage, long-term debt, or warrants on shares in treasury, all of them fictions.

And why should we care?

Because "ownership" is one of the latter. It is *not* a real thing, but a fictional one. So before delving deeper, here's a first important observation.

CFA TYPES IGNORE NOT JUST PEOPLE, BUT PHYSICAL STUFF TOO

If you do *security* analysis (an analysis of fictional names, mostly on the balance sheet's right), you're in CFA mode: price to book value, debt/equity ratio, retained earnings, warrants on shares in treasury, all these items have no *physicality* behind them. But because such an analysis can be done at one's desk, with pen and paper, or a keyboard, and a cup of coffee—and without leaving the room—many "investors" do them, happily computing and re-computing them, but with very little payoff—as the list of underperformers in the Introduction proves.

That is: because computing these fictions is easy, all intellectual investors do them, and so these items' utility often vanishes.

But what about the left side, the physical one? What does it include?

ALL THINGS ARE ON A BALANCE SHEET SOMEWHERE

Ah. Just look around you.

If you are at the office, look down the hall; or if you are at home, gaze through the window down the street. Everything you see before you, everything *physical*, is owned by someone (real), or something (fictional): desks, chairs, pianos, cars, houses, bicycles, trees, shoes, watches, everything physical is listed on someone's (or something's) balance sheet's *left* side as an *asset*, and so is "owned" by this someone or something (a fictional entity like a company, or a partnership, or a trust, or a city or a country. All of them fictional, yes).

EVERYTHING PHYSICAL IS OWNED

In point of fact, everything on earth (and also in near space) is *owned* by someone or something, and so sits on a balance sheet somewhere. The only exceptions are people (which no longer can be owned), wild animals, and the occasional patches of jungle—but even the latter are owned by the local government—which is a fiction also, as noted above.

So finally, again, what *is* ownership?

OWNERSHIP IS A FICTION WITH THREE KEY ASPECTS

Ownership is a human fiction with three unique aspects: *benefit, control,* and *transferability*. Without all three, it isn't really ownership. You should re-read the last sentence until it sinks in, because if you neglect even one of these three aspects, you won't get rich.

Due to their extreme importance, here are these three again, in further detail:

1. Benefit *is the power (accepted by the community, as per the law) to use or enjoy an asset exclusively*—e.g., the ability to relax in your condo, which, in order to let you enjoy it, is coupled with the power to kick out homeless squatters from it. This power is called "*enforceability*," and it too is accepted by the community. *Without it, ownership is meaningless.*

We'll get to that again when we mention investing in foreign countries or foreign stock markets.

2. Control *is the power to decide who besides you can, and who cannot, benefit from your asset*—e.g., your children, your girlfriend (or boyfriend), a paying renter—but *not* the homeless, as per above. That, too, depends on enforceability.

3. Finally, ***transferability*** *is the power to sell the "benefit and control" powers* to someone (or something) else—the new owner. This, too, must be accepted by the community, and be enforceable by law. So yet again: No enforceability, no transferability, and no ownership. (We'll see this again, below, under the heading of "corruption.")

These triple requirements are what ownership means: I wrote about it in my first book also, but am repeating it here because it's so crucial to all that you aim for as a sleuth. Thus, *if you want to own more, you'll have to understand deeply what ownership means.* Only if you understand all three parts can you begin to invest better—and also sleuth better, as you'll subdivide your sleuthing targets into these three categories. Look it up again in my first book.

PHYSICAL EXAMPLE FOR A FICTIONAL "OWNERSHIP"

Let's take an example. Your home (if you have one) is on your balance sheet's left side. Say a 200 m^2, two-story split-level house, on the corner of First and Main, owned by you.

What does it mean, *a house owned by you*?

OWNERSHIP: THE MAGIC OF MOVING A JUDGE TO SEND A BAILIFF

It means your ownership is proven by an ink squiggle on a document called a "title deed." Yes, your ownership is fictional, a communal state-of-mind, but the "title deed" can be either real (a stamped paper document at the Title Office) or fictional too (encrypted blips on a screen at the Title Office.) Let's leave this alone for now and continue with your balance sheet.

Your home is noted as an asset on the left side, under Assets. But your net ownership, after debt, your net wealth, is at the bottom of the right page, under Owner's Equity.

The term "Equity" is just as fictional as the term ownership, and is a matter of accounting formula, that is, ink squiggles. Yet it has very real power, because *the title deed is based on the magical ability to move a judge to send in a bailiff,* in case someone squatted on your property. (Unless, some would say, you are in San Francisco or in Paris, because there, squatters seemingly can stay forever.)

AGAIN: WITHOUT ENFORCEABILITY THERE'S NO OWNERSHIP

Without that magic power of enforceability, i.e., the power to send the bailiff to kick a squatter out, your ownership is worth zip. To "own" anything, you *must* have the power to move a judge to send a bailiff, who'll kick out the interloper. And the judge must be movable *only* by your title deed, not by the squatter's gun, or money, or politician-father.

All these other causes either negate your ownership, or dilute it considerably.

If however, the above caveat holds (incorruptible judges), then this power of yours—or of any owner—to move a judge is called the rule of law, which is a powerful magic indeed. Since **without it, there is no**

property, no ownership of either homes or stocks and/or bonds, and no enjoyment of private things at all.

Without this power, anyone with a bigger gun than yours can take your home, any homeless horde larger than your family can invade your condo, renters can refuse to pay rent or get out, and *stocks in the market become pieces of toilet paper, if the ruler so decrees.*

Yes, like "stocks" in China, or Russia, or any other countries where the rule of law is absent. In such places, value investing, indeed *any* investing, is meaningless. Contra Warren and Charlie who "invest" in China, yes. And contra Jimmy Rogers, who "invests" in Russia. But, perhaps to your surprise, Brazil is OK, despite the mayhem and the crime, and so is Mexico, maybe. Lebanon is a maybe too. But it is a no for Egypt, and a no for Saudi Arabia.

Now, before we go to two real cases that illuminate the power of sleuthing on the balance sheet's left, and the power of ownership, let's skip back for a minute to your balance sheet. Your physical asset (home) is on the left, above, and your equity is on the right, below.

What else is on the right?

LIABILITIES CAN MAKE OWNERSHIP CONDITIONAL

Under liabilities, right above equity, you can see "long-term debt," or a "claim" on your home, by the bank that owns a mortgage on your house.

Yes, the bank *owns* the mortgage, just like you own your home.

In both cases, this "own" is a legal claim—meaning, a right (yes, another fiction) accepted by anyone in the country who obeys the law. That is, the bank's mortgage claim will be accepted by a judge also, without fear of bribery or pressure, if you don't meet your monthly payments.

The meaning of the latter is that debt *reduces* your "net ownership," and although it doesn't cancel it, it also makes it *conditional.* That's because if you don't pay the mortgage, the bank (the mortgage owner) can ask a judge to send a bailiff to evict *you.*

Which means that, if one has debt secured by one's assets, then one's ownership is conditional upon meeting one's interest obligations.

UNPAID DEBT MEANS OWNERSHIP'S VALUE CAN FALL, EVEN TO ZERO

It is the same for companies regarding the assets they own, if they have lots of debt. The more debt they have, the less secure their ownership. In the extreme, the company may undergo bankruptcy, in which case the assets it owns (and which is the main reason you own the stock) are given to the lender, and your stock would fall a lot, maybe even to zero.

All this, of course, is predicated on the assumption that the judges in that country are not crooked. Because if they are, there really is no real ownership, debt or no debt.

And now let's go to two case-studies where both these concepts, seeking value on the left side of the balance sheet, and ownership rights, are demonstrated.

CASE 1. HOW TO SLEUTH FOR VALUE ON THE LEFT

Assume you've found a company whose assets you like, but whose stock (you suspect) is undervalued, due to its less-than-stellar management that detracts from operations.

How much is the stock really worth?

As a sleuth, your instinct is to go where no other investor has gone before. Yes, even in the financial statements. But where?

You then remember to stick to the left side of the balance sheet—the *physical* asset side—and so you look there, and lo! You see that the company owns real estate. Say it owns the land under its office building, which is at the intersection of Second and Main, Pleasantville.

The real estate is carried (as at year-end, three months before) at a value of $125 million, which is a combination of land, building, improvements, and suchlike.

Hmm, you say. But how much is it *really* worth? Remember, this land is physical reality. Not an accounting term. The real thing. Physically.

So how do you go about finding out its real value?

SLEUTHING REAL VALUE

If you are an intellectual CFA investor, you may print out the footnotes, re-read them, see the address, the acreage, the location, then go click-click to a real estate database, to see what similar properties had sold for during the last year or two or three. You then calculate the price per acre, per sq ft of office space, price per number of stories, per proximity to City Hall, or whatever other data is in the databases, that the publisher states as significant.

Data that someone *else* had put in, that is. And that *others* have probably seen already.

So that's one way. Analysis of public information, using logic. That is, "System 2" thinking. Nothing wrong with it. But also, of course, nothing right. Because if you do that, you are still in the land of ink squiggles and screen blips, info known to everyone else.

So how can you dig out physical info by yourself?

Say the building is in a neglected area of downtown, and no equivalent piece of real estate has sold near there for the last three years.

How would a sleuth go about it?

THE SLEUTH GOES PHYSICAL

First, you copy the address to a piece of paper (not to your cell: you stay physical), then turn off your computer and walk (or drive) to that address, and meander around it on foot. You note what condition the building is in. The neighborhood, too. Is it winos and homeless hiccupping on corners, or posh streets smelling of rosehip tea? Is it an Army and Navy store and a row of pawnshops, or a fancy Zara handbags emporium?

You return to the building and see it has a multi-level mall with shops. You go in and chat to the shop owners. You let drop you're considering opening a store here. What can they tell you about the landlord?

Some will tell, others won't. If they can't talk because they're busy, that's data in itself. If they are free and still don't want to talk, that's data too.

Or maybe they do talk? Depends on your questions.

STORE OWNERS ARE OFTEN A SOURCE OF INFO

For example, you ask: How long has your store been here? What's the average tenure of a store? Why so short / so long? Has the traffic climbed last year? Or has it fallen? And, how is the landlord in general? Do they clean the mall well? Any security issues? How are store thefts? Burglaries? Teenager rampages? How fast does the police respond? Any, ahem, young men selling chemicals?

Maybe the store owners answer, maybe they don't. But you'll get some info. And as you get it, you begin to learn what questions to ask, both in this sleuthing, and in future ones.

BANKS MAY BE SOURCES TOO

Is there a bank branch in the mall? If so, talk to them too. Same questions, but also others: talk to the manager. Say you're considering opening up a store here. Does the bank have a service for store owners in this branch, or is it all handled from uptown?

Go all around the mall, up and down the building, through the staircases, to other levels, if there are any. See what other tenants are there. That's the building's cash flow. See the underground parking. Is it well-lit or dark? Are there many cars? Clean ones? New, or ancient? If there's a police station in the area, go in and ask them too. It's unlikely they'd talk freely, but you never know. And, you can always send your assistant, who is comely (but has a black belt in kung fu also), to talk to the constables. Maybe she can make them talk? If she does, she can get a bonus.

POST-SLEUTHING CONSULTATIONS WITH PROS

Finally, you go back to the office, note down all you've asked, the gist of the answers, and ideas that have come to mind from these. Then you look for *the best industrial real estate agent in town.* Or, alternatively, the *best real estate lawyer in town.*

If you don't know who they are, call the real estate board and the local lawyers' association, and ask. Or, if you have friends in real estate, ask for introductions. The latter are usually best.

How do you know the names you are given are the best?

Simple. They are the most expensive. These are the ones you want.

Then, if you are a private investor, you call them up and set up a meeting. If you work for a large pension fund, say, you call them up and give your name and the name of your employer. Few professionals would spurn a potential new client.

Say it's a real estate lawyer you are meeting.

MEETING WITH A TOP PRO

You go in, and ask: What is the real value of that piece of land + the building that company XYZ office is sitting on, on Second and Main?

The top real estate lawyer in town would be able to tell you this, right off the bat. You'll of course pay his or her fee, which could be a grand or two, for an hour of consultation.

How would the top lawyer know that value?

Because the top lawyer or top industrial real estate agent knows all this by heart. There are books (today there are databases) that tell you Who owns What in Pleasantville (or NYC, or San Fran, or LA), but they rarely reflect the latest, and certainly not the scuttlebutt, which, like Phil Fisher, is what you are after.

If the lawyer (or real estate agent) doesn't know, then he or she is not high enough, and you must look for someone better, higher, and more expensive.

Oh yes, of course, all this will cost you. *All good sleuthing will cost.* Sleuthing isn't freebie screen-blips on Twitter, where anyone who offers their worthless views for free is a genius. This is the physical, real world, where truth is exclusive, time-consuming, and *doesn't* come free.

Why time-consuming?

Because it will take you time to get to the real sources. As they say on Wall Street, those who talk don't know, and those who know don't talk. (At least not for free.)

Now say you've gotten into a conversation with the top real estate lawyer. He tells you that this piece of land belonging to XYZ Corp is worth at least $500 million, perhaps more, because of rumored plans to construct a tower over it.

Rumored how? Rumored where?

Oh, he says vaguely, City Hall scuttlebutt and such. Nothing certain.

(To get to this point, however, you may have to spend an hour or more just establishing trust. Such scuttlebutt isn't free. You pay both with money and with info, and also with time, during which your interlocutor can sniff out whether or not you are trustworthy.)

But, you say, Co. XYZ carries the land and building on the books for a mere $125 million.

The lawyer laughs deeply. Oh, yes, he says. Sure. But they have a mortgage against it.

Only $50 million mortgage, you say (because you've read the footnotes). Why don't they note the real value too?

Oh, the lawyer says, and winks. Probably screw-up insurance.

What's that? you ask.

He says, That's in case Co. XYZ management screws up and needs money, they can then mortgage up the property. (And indeed, they've screwed up plenty already, or their stock wouldn't be that cheap. And they wouldn't have that $50 million mortgage.)

Ah, you say. So if we can buy their property for anything less than $200 or $250 million, we're good?

Oh, says the lawyer, do you want to buy it?

Not at the moment, you say. I'm just doing the analysis for my boss, who runs the real estate portfolio.

Ah, says the lawyer. If you need some professional due diligence done...

Maybe in future, you say. So $250 million may get it?

SLEUTHING BEGINS TO DISCOVER VALUE

Not on your life, says the lawyer. They'll never let it go for less than $500 million, and maybe not even then.

Not even $500 million?! Why not?

The lawyer looks at you pityingly and says, Because XYZ's managers own very few shares in the company, as I'm sure you saw in the filings, why should they sell it? They're paid a salary and a bonus, maybe some piddling options. So if the stock goes up $5, so what? They own very little.

Ah, you say. Then you ask a few more bland questions, leave your card (you'd better have one), thank the lawyer, sign a check for one grand (if he wants it on the spot), and go back to the office. (Assuming you are with a pension fund or other such institution.)

What now?

Now you call Co. XYZ's switchboard, and say you are with Pension Fund Y, and say you would like to talk to the CFO, or the Controller. If they fob you off to Investor Relations, don't be discouraged. You'll get to the CFO soon enough.

Assume you talk to Investor Relations (anyone can talk to them), then what you say is this: I am an analyst (or a portfolio manager) at Plumbers Mutual Re-Insurance (let's say), and I am calling about your property on Second and Main. Who should I talk to?

VALUE-PROOF BEGINS

Why are you calling? says the flack.

We may have an interest in it, for the right price. Who should I talk to?

You would then very probably be able to talk to the CFO or the treasurer. Eventually.

Then what you say is this (or something like it). And please pay attention to the words:

I am an analyst at Plumbers Re doing a valuation of properties for our real estate portfolio. I was asked to do analysis of your Second and Main property, which you carry at a value of $125 million. Now, on a non-held basis, without any obligation on our part or yours, if we were to express a formal interest in it, and were to make a formal offer, what sort of number would get your attention?

Now if there's value in the property well beyond the $125 million, you are likely to be fobbed off.

In such a case you call again, and say that if you were considering making a formal offer to the board, sent by registered mail tomorrow 10:00 a.m., just to avoid wasting everybody's time, what sort of number would get their attention?

POWER PLAY BEGINS

Let's pause here. Because this, dear reader, is power play.

You have just put in a notional, conditional bid, and are probing for a notional, conditional ask. (Before you do, of course, your boss had better be informed. But if he's an ambitious capitalist, he'd probably love it.)

Yet, if the property is really worth $500 million+, XYZ's people will likely tell you not to bother, they are not interested in selling.

But at what price would you be? you ask. $600 million? More?

No interest, they say. No need to send us a letter.

Now let's pause again. Why don't they want a letter?

Because, once / if the board gets a formal offer, *they are legally obligated to consider it*, and respond. And if they clearly don't want to... Maybe it really is worth more?...

Well, well.

This is a good place to pause and mention Carl Icahn again. Because that's usually the mode of operation of active value investors like him: **Active investors immediately look at the balance sheet's left side, and try to dig out the real value.**

Not the right side, where accounting jiggery pokery or fancy footnote perusal may discover some pennies' value missed by the 35 million other CFA intellectuals who have perused it at their desks. With coffee, and A.C., and perhaps some soft music in the background.

No. As a sleuth, you stay on the left side. The real, physical side. And do real physical work on the list of assets. Physical. Outside. No music, no A.C.

And talk to pros who know, and pay them.

Like this:

CASE 2. AN EXAMPLE OF SHORTS, STILL WITH CARL ICAHN

When Bill Ackman foolishly went public with his short position in Herbalife (HLF), Carl Icahn wanted to see how much it was really worth, and if the biz was as near-criminal as Ackman was muttering about it in public.

But how to find this out? Asking Wall Street analysts? Look up valuations on the Internet?

Piffle. Carl Icahn did neither. He didn't go into databases and didn't go click-click calc-calc, nor did he send any of his dozen analysts to do so. Like a proper sleuth, he did it all himself. He called the top consumer product lawyer in NYC, and asked him about it.

No, said the top c.p. lawyer. HLF is not criminal. Yes, it's a skanky biz, making the distributors buy their vitamin inventories, but payday loan co's, or grade C credit card co's are skankier, and so are most pawnbrokers. But so fiddling what? HLF's cash flow is good, and the biz is steady. Yeah, management is not the best, but they don't have to be. The biz runs itself, practically. And it spins off cash. Why are you asking?

Oh, Carl Icahn said, I heard there's a big short position in the stock. What about management there? Not the best, you said?

Then came half an hour of internal industry gossip, both unreportable and unrepeatable, that the c.p. lawyer was happy to share, for a grand or two of billable time. Also, he knew Icahn would not repeat it. And did I say he (the lawyer) was being paid?

So far so good. Then, just to be sure, a day later, Icahn called the second-best consumer product lawyer, and got a similar opinion. The entire sleuthing probably cost him three or four grand. Bubkes.

And then, finally, he went and bought a ton of HLF shares, *and registered their ownership*. To his own company. Normally people own shares via the broker. That is, the broker owns the shares, so he can lend them to a short seller, on which loan he (the broker) earns interest. But if the owner registers the shares, the broker-held shares cannot be loaned without the registered owner's permission.

Which of course Icahn didn't give. (See ownership's three attributes again.) And then he sat back to gloat (discreetly).

Why did Icahn gloat? Because by boasting, Ackman basically cut his own throat, telling the entire world he was short, practically inviting others to buy the shares and register them. Unless they considered the shares too risky to own, that is. Which Icahn just found was not the case, by sleuthing it. And so, now that Icahn owned the shares, he could dictate that they not be loaned. And they of course weren't.

And when others learned of this, they too bought the shares and registered them, piggybacking on Carl Icahn's coattails. And they too forbade lending.

Again, see above for the definition of ownership and its benefits.

The entire affair ended with Ackman having to close his short (i.e., buy back his borrowed shares) at a big loss, because he did the short wrong, and Icahn did his sleuthing right.

DOING THINGS RIGHT, VS. DOING THE RIGHT THINGS

Now you may ask: If Icahn did things right, why then did he underperform the market over the last 15 years?

Because, although he does his sleuthing right, in my view he often applies it to the not-quite-right deals. Herbalife was well-sleuthed, yes, but it was still an opportunistic short-term investment. Luckily it was not Icahn's usual mode of operation, but it was frequent enough to render the use of his considerable talents non-optimal. Carl Icahn probably should have stuck to long-term investing in truly superior companies (which, to be fair, do form the large part of his portfolio.)

Why did Icahn veer away from pure long-term investing, a la Buffett and Munger?

Because, as a born showman, he probably just loves the drama of a turnaround. And I know of what I speak: I have a similar failing. I did one turnaround (a brokerage company), and helped in another (a Tech, mentioned in *TSI*). And I can testify that although both were exciting and fun, in retrospect the drama and effort were barely worth it, because they ate up my time, which might've been better used for sleuthing more deeply into boring but truly great companies, that do *not* get into trouble.

Nine times out of ten, a company gets into trouble not just because of management error, but because its business is mediocre. (See Chapter 7 for how to find the truly superior ones.) So even when the trouble is fixed, and the company survives, the in-built mediocrity remains. Like Herbalife's.

My advice: Avoid turnarounds. Get your drama and fun elsewhere.

CASE 3. ON A PERSONAL NOTE

The real estate sleuthing method, by the way, is based on real life:

When I was with Gordon Capital, the Canadian institutional broker / merch banker that changed Canadian finance, we used such methods to break the old boys' club of underwriting.

At the time, when a Canadian company wanted to sell shares, its CFO went to his old-boy chums on Bay Street, who then sold the new shares on a "best-efforts" basis. So the price the company got for the shares was never the best, and existing shareholders, including the apocryphal widows and orphans, were thereby shortchanged.

Gordon decided there's opportunity there, and got third parties to backstop us, so when we learned that a company might be interested in selling shares, we sent our best analyst to sleuth them to make sure the shares were worth it, and then we gave the directors a firm offer.

They of course hated it, because this meant that their broker chums would have to bid firm also, which they didn't have the cojones for, nor the capital.

The way we did it was to send a registered letter with an offer to the board and registered copies to every director, which meant they had to act on it, because if they didn't, they'd incur a legal liability. Personally.

Soon enough, Gordon Capital changed the underwriting biz in Canada. In fact, we brought it into the 20th century, because underwriting really means you take on the risk. Old boy brokers didn't. We did. But it had to be done by coercing directors to do the right thing. Same in the little fictional fable above.

And by the way, the above is also good for passive investors. Because if you owned shares in Co. XYZ, and then found out that their real estate is carried at one-third of its real value, you could then publicize the fact by telling an ambitious, junior Wall Street or Bay Street analyst (or two). They could then make a name for themselves with clients for their research, and thereby also acquire clout with the company who'd fear them for their thoroughness.

And in the future, these analysts may also act as Wall Street sources for you.

See?

WHAT ARE THE SLEUTHING LESSONS IN THIS CHAPTER?

First, when sleuthing for value, go **left** on the balance sheet.

Second, go **physical**, and go **yourself**.

Third, go to **real experts** and ask them about the biz, and about the people.

Finally, and fourth, **pay** them, and—most important—**keep your mouth shut**.

And just to make it complete, here are some general *conclusions & implications:*

Financial statements are only a model of business and miss a lot of the real, physical thing.

Accounting ignores people who drive the numbers (or destroy them). You shouldn't.

The balance sheet is **half real** (the left side), **half fiction** (the right). **Focus on the left, physical side**, sleuth it physically, and you'll take CFAs' money.

Watch out for any problem in ownership. Its three rules must be cast-iron. Both for the stock itself, and for the legal jurisdiction it is under.

CHAPTER 2

HISTORIANS' POINT OF VIEW

Who created whom: history or leaders? Company or managers?

Now, what *other* kind of edge can you get over stay-on-the-screen CFAs?

Obviously, it has to do with the *other* blindness of accounting: *People*, that basic component of corporations, nowhere to be seen in the financial statements.

So maybe you should focus on them.

OK, but focus how?

Let's see. Since corporations are *commercial* groups competing with each other, perhaps we could look at history, which is *political* groups vying with each other. After all, both companies and countries are *groups in conflict*, led by leaders both competent and not.

And if this analogy is valid, then maybe historians' methods of forecasting *historical* events could help you forecast *market* events as well?

It's worth a shot.

After all, there's a lot of data about countries' history, both in times of peace and of war. And, similarly, there's plenty of data about *companies'* history, both successes and failures, as reflected in their financial statements.

Could we then, for this purpose, see companies' financial statements as their histories?

Assuming we can, let's see where this gets us, starting with history's prime question.

DO LEADERS MAKE HISTORY, OR DOES HISTORY MAKE LEADERS?

When Napoleon invaded Russia in June 1812, the Russian army under General Kutuzov kept retreating, purposefully drawing Napoleon's half a million troops deeper into Russia's snowy interior. But as Napoleon's soldiers reached Moscow, they found it in flames: General Kutuzov had given orders to burn the city down so as to deny the enemy shelter or provisions.

With no one to fight, and no shelter or food for his soldiers, and snow falling, Napoleon eventually retreated all the way back to Paris, losing 90% of his army on the way.

When Kutuzov was later complimented on his ingenious "scorched earth" strategy, he declined the praise. *Any other general, he said, would have made the same decision.*

Or that, at least, is how the Russian writer Leo Tolstoy describes it in his book *War and Peace*.

TOLSTOYAN VIEW OF HISTORY: LEADERS DON'T MATTER

This extreme point of view is therefore called the *Tolstoyan view of history*: leaders do not make history. Rather, history makes leaders by *forcing* them to obey its diktat.

But is this really so? Don't leaders' decisions matter? After all, many leaders *do* have choices. And what's more, there is proof of such a view:

In his recent book, *Undelivered*, author Jeff Nussbaum cites a large number of ungiven speeches by political leaders who did face such a choice—and Nussbaum should know. He has written speeches for several US presidents and presidential aspirants, and so had a ringside seat in history's kitchen as leaders pondered their decisions—when these mattered.

But, yes, sometimes they didn't matter.

For example, before elections, leaders usually have their writers compose two speeches, one for each potential outcome. In a democracy, voters have the last say so the choice of the speech is up to history, thus perhaps supporting the Tolstoyan view.

However, the practice of composing two speeches is also prevalent in other cases, where a leader *does* have a choice, but simply has not yet made it. In such cases, Nussbaum's "undelivered speeches" are living proofs that—on many occasions—leaders do indeed make history happen.

DOSTOEVSKY'S VIEW OF HISTORY: LEADERS MAKE IT HAPPEN

So no, Tolstoy's view of history is not the only one among historians.

Fyodor Dostoevsky, the other great Russian writer, holds the opposite view. In his book *Crime and Punishment* he tells of a moral choice made by an individual that indeed mattered. Dostoevsky's view is therefore the opposite to Tolstoy's: leaders do make history, not the other way around.

And that's why historians' debate about whether leaders or history are history's prime engine is often referred to as Tolstoy's view of history vs. Dostoevsky's.

SAME AS CFA'S VS. SLEUTHS?

And just why does all this matter for you as a sleuth investor?

Because *that very same question is found implicitly in investors' approach to stocks.*

CFAs and other intellectual investors fall squarely in Tolstoy's camp: Only the financial situation matters (they implicitly say), by dictating management actions, while the leaders' abilities and flaws do not. The proof of their implied view is that corporate leaders' names do not even appear in any of the company's three accounting statements. A Steve Jobs would not be an asset, nor a former IBM chairman a liability.

Or, see also O'Shaughnessy's book, where buys/sells are purely equated with numerical cheapness, no names of leaders needed. Even hallowed pioneers like Ben Graham treat the company as mere numbers, in his Net-Net rules, or Working Capital per share.

Sleuths, on the other hand, fall more (though not exclusively) in Dostoevsky's camp: Yes, they admit that numbers (financial statements) do matter, but leaders matter too, and often even more.

CFA'S VS. SLEUTHS: HOW WOULD EACH TREAT IACOCCA?

So, whose view is more right than the other?

It cannot be the CFAs', because, if it is, how to account for Lee Iacocca? Lee had become the CEO of a bankrupt Chrysler, whose value was negative (meager assets, huge and growing liabilities), but in a few years made it into a $2 billion market cap company.

One man, $2 billion difference.

Could Chrysler's Value Line one-page have foreseen Chrysler's miraculous resurrection, without mentioning Iacocca's name? At the very least, Lee's name should've appeared as an asset on Chrysler's balance sheet, just as Steve Jobs' name should have appeared on Apple's, or Bill Gates' on Microsoft's—or, yes, Warren Buffett's and Charlie Munger's on Berkshire's.

Or, on the other hand, just to mention the opposite case: perhaps IBM's management and board of a decade ago should have appeared as liabilities on theirs?

So, yet again: How should you treat leaders' abilities and flaws when you are trying to forecast the stock performance of the company they lead? Do they matter only in extremes? And how to judge those if they are not analyzable in numbers and categories?

CAN YOU GET STOCK-PICKING TIPS FROM HISTORY?

Let's see now:

Perhaps if we consider financial statements as akin to a stock's corporate history, we can pick tips from real history about how to treat a stock and company analysis, by divining when to be more Tolstoyan, when more Dostoevskyan.

And, most important for your goal of outperforming: Can we learn from history how to sleuth that *extra* people-information that does *not* appear in the financial statement? And perhaps even get ideas about where to get it, and how?

COMPARING FINANCIAL HISTORY TO REAL HISTORY

To see that, let's conduct a thought experiment of forecasting the outcome of a *historical conflict* and see what it can teach us about analyzing *commercial* conflict—for that, after all, is what stock markets are.

AN INTEL ANALYST VS. A STOCK ANALYST

Imagine you are an intelligence analyst working for the Bureau of National Defense, known as the BND, for a middle European country we shall call Germonia.

Your boss hands you a VL (Very Latest) summary of the last 20 years' finances of two neighboring countries, Ukronia and Russonia.

The two countries are of different sizes (Russonia is bigger), and so are their armies. Russonia has more cannons and tanks, while Ukronia has more battle tractors and home-made missile-drones. As for infantry, both have about the same numbers, although R's soldiers are 45% drunker and U's 35% better educated. And oh yes, Russonia has 3,000 Kryptonite bombs while Ukronia doesn't, yet the UN frowns on their use.

Is this all we have? you ask your boss.

No, he says. We also have this, and he hands you more printout pages. Here are the two countries' figures for GDP (R's is 3x U's), GDP per capita (both are tiny, the size of Bulgaria's, or Togo's), percent of assets owned by oligarchs (similar), % of corruption (ditto), total defense spending, total income taxes, tons of food stored, % taxes paid or avoided...

In short, *anything expressible in numbers and categories* you can have. Whatever isn't countable or categorizable is considered mushy, and is only given cursorily. This entire trove of data and some mushy stuff is stored in five large IBM computer disks, accessible at a click. You are given the encryption key.

How good is the data? you ask.

As good as it can be, says your boss. And here are some more mushy estimates based on theories by boffins in our back office, and some satellite pictures, and a list of rumors. By the way, all data is audited for accuracy by Arthur Andersen & Company.

I am joking of course, the boss says, when he sees you gawp. It's audited by the United Nations. OK, I'm still joking. It has been audited by Jimmy

Carter, a below-average former US president but a saintly person with above-average honesty, who is a friend of our Prime Minister's pastor. So you can trust the data as far as you can trust JC.

And what is my mission? you ask.

TWO-LAYERED MARCHING ORDERS

It is this, your boss says: These two countries (R and U) are about to go to war with each other over disputed territory containing sorghum, kryptonite deposits, and elk-dung fertilizer. Just like Pepsi and Coke are warring over market share of Organic Cola. And by the way, says the boss, the presidents of both U and R have declared confidently that they'll win.

And? you ask. Which of the two do we support?

Ahh, your boss says: First, our government would like to know who is more likely to win.

Why do we need this info? you ask.

Because, the boss says, the Germonian cabinet needs to know which of the two governments, R or U, to suck up to more—the one more likely to win—and which to distance itself from publicly—the one more likely to lose. It's in the long-term national interest. And by the way, your boss adds, the Franconian Government is going through the same process, for the same purpose. But keep it under your hat.

Yawohl, you say, as you turn to leave.

But just before you go, your boss narrows his eyes and adds: Also, we need to know if the winner may win *too* decisively, because if that winner is R, we'll have to do some extra sucking up to them, which we can do. But if it's U, they can become too big for their breeches and then they'd compete with us for sucking up to the Murikonians, which we already do too much of.

I see, you say. And did all this come from the VL numbers?

No, says your boss. It never does. That's why we need people like you.

You don't really like his tone of voice, but as a well-trained analyst you say, Understood. Yes, of course. Who will win, and by how much, and who by too much, if any.

Yah, says your boss, you got it. We're relying on you. Go to it.

You then depart, eager to do your job.

But how should you go about it?

IS ALL DATA INFORMATION?

Do you have enough information? You certainly have enough *data*. But is it also *information*? And even if so, is it the *right* kind? What's the right kind of information, anyway, what's the wrong kind? And what about that last bit, that answers you are asked for cannot be gotten from the numbers? Where from, then? And what does "people like you" mean?

But first, the data: What is the right kind?

Obviously, *the right data is the kind to which success or failure can be attributed.* But attributed how? From your accounting courses, and also from a brief summer seminar in history, you remember that the problem of attribution is notoriously hard. What really causes victory? What causes defeat? And can such causes (if such can indeed be found) be expressed in numbers only?

And even if so, how do you know which of the numbers in Germonia's VL database are relevant? And, perhaps as critical, is there any information that the giant database does *not* contain, that *is* relevant?

IS THE RIGHT INFORMATION MEASURABLE?

For example: What about the characters of the *leaders* of both sides? Is either of them a Chrysler's Lee Iacocca type? Or, on the other hand, is either of them an IBM former chairman type? Or a Jimmy Carter type?

There are a few sketchy views about both leaders by Murikonian psychologists: The R leader is seen as a corrupt, competent killer with 7 mistresses, 9 children, and 97 murders to his credit, while the U leader is seen as a charismatic, inexperienced, honest, family-type idiot.

But are they right? How to find out? Or is it really worth your time to try? Isn't your time better spent in correlating the number of tanks and ammo rounds? Either task, whether tanks or leaders, will take time, which is now at a premium. The Germonian cabinet is waiting, and your job is on the line.

Alright, then. That's as far as the fable of historical forecast can go for now. We'll get back to it later, but first, please switch hats.

FINANCIAL STATEMENTS AS HISTORY OF CORPORATE WARS

You are now on Wall Street, a research analyst at a leading investment boutique, specializing in consumer leisure beverages. Your job is to forecast earnings of entertaining drink companies, and issue stock buys and sells to Institutional Investors (II) who run large portfolios of OPM (Other People's Money). If your work is good (that is, prescient enough), the IIs will do more of their trading of entertaining drink stocks through your employer, and you'll get a bonus. Which you need, since your wife just had twins.

However, now you have an additional task, besides forecasting earnings.

A CORPORATE WAR BREAKS OUT

Just last month, Pepsi's new chairwoman declared she was going to fight Coke for Organic Cola market share in Europe, aiming at the large African immigrant market.

Your boss, the research director, hands you the assignment: Which of the two behemoth companies is likely to win this market-share battle over the next 3–5 years?

If you can come up with a convincing answer, II clients of your boutique who run a lot of OPM will do much more trading through your employer, and you'll get an extra bonus. Which you sure could use.

However, this is a new kind of task, not just an earnings forecasts but a battle-win forecast. What will you base it on?

FORECASTING CORPORATE WAR RESULTS

Assume you have all the financial / numerical Value Line files of both PEP and KO, as well as their financial data filed with the SEC in its EDGAR database going thirty years back. You also have Compustat's restatement of the numbers.

In other words, you know these companies as well as can be imagined—but *viewed as numbers only*. Nothing else, except of course the names of the accounting categories being reported as numbers.

And oh, yes: You also have all the computing power you want, and all the cheap labor of MBA and CFA interns who'd work for next to nothing, just to add a line to their resumes.

And yes, yes, you also have access to hundreds of programs of regression analysis, and Neural Networks, genetic algorithms, and anything else in MIT's library of forecasting software, to which your employer subscribes.

So you gather your notes, retire to your office, and spread the detailed financial statements on the desk before you. Besides the financial statements there are also lots of ratios, computed by the database for both companies. There are Current Ratios and P/E ratios and Debt/Equity ratios, all done to three decimals, and something called Q-Ratios, which comes from Japan, and also EV/EBITDA ratios on a weekly basis. And yes, there are also charts, which come in Candlesticks and Hi-Lo-Close format and in colors, with moving average superimposed, as well as regression lines and something called an Ichimoku cloud, which yes, comes from Japan too.

In other words, any information which is numerical and categorical that can be stored in ink and bits and blips, you can have.

The question is:

Can you produce a reasonably reliable forecast about which company will likely win the organic cola market share battle, and if so, how decisively, and so, presumably, its stock should be a long, the other a short?

Yes? No? If the latter, what are you missing?

NUMERICAL DATA LACKS FUTURE PLANS

First of all, you miss the war plans of both companies. Or rather, both their offensive and defensive aspects. You don't have these because the companies keep them secret, and of course there's nothing about them in the financial statements, because these reflect the *past*, and are *facts*, even though only of the numerical kind, whereas the battle plans concern the *future*, which hasn't yet happened, and are in words of intention instead of numbers, i.e., fictions in the leaders' minds. So now both companies, pre-commercial war, are pregnant with possible futures, really like a particle's wave function before it has collapsed into a single category when an observer has applied a measurement to it. (As we'll see in the chapter on physics.)

You idly wonder: Is this observer you?

But if so, and let's say you did manage to divine the two companies' strategies and published them: Would this cause a change in them, and so perhaps render your forecast false? Perhaps even flip the outcome?

At the risk of disorientation, put on the BND intel analyst's hat again.

Oddly, you have the exact same worry: Is the future of the R – U war somehow dependent on your findings? And if so, how to incorporate it into your calculations?

Yet again, switch hats to an analyst's fedora:

Even forgetting about your potential impact on corporate battle plans: How to go about your analysis? Did you miss anything? For example, how good are the opposing leaders at making war? *How good are they at generating success?*

What to do, then?

ARE BATTLE FORECASTS A MATTER OF NUMBERS ONLY?

Let's discard both hats and pause here.

Because as you probably realize, the Pepsi / Coke assignment is almost directly comparable to the one before, of forecasting which country, U or R, would win the territory-share battle. There, too, you have lots of numerical data about the past and the present, but very little about future battle plans, or about the ability of their respective chiefs, and their generals, and their militaries and supporting economies, to conduct a battle and win.

And by the way, regarding battles: What of their supporting allies, if any? And their suppliers, of both money and weapons (that is, for R and U, not PEP and KO), or perhaps extra people?

Should you consider these too? How could you not? And if so, how?

So once again: Do you have all the data to make a war forecast? In either case? Commercial or military?

Clearly not.

Why not? What's missing in addition to the above?

LOOKING FOR HELP

Let's put your boffin hat on again (one last time) and go back to the BND office. You are again an intel analyst trying to solve the R vs. U problem.

Since the answer would form part of history, you lay aside the databases and reach for your bookshelf, to see if history can perhaps guide you on your BND assignment.

We already saw that historians can be divided roughly into Tolstoyans and Dostoevskyans.

Are there (among either category) any recognized *experts on making historical predictions*?

Well, it seems there are several such, and all have strong opinions.

SOME HISTORICAL PREDICTORS

Let's go first to old Karl Marx.

Marx (another categorizer) said that a country has three ingredients for success: land, capital, and labor. By land, by the way, he meant both land and natural resources. So yes, in the case of U and R, we have data for all three. We have lists of natural resources both current and historical (and also some forecasts), data of capital (i.e., money) resources, as well as data for workforce—which can be seen as fighting force too.

So: Can we use these Marxian triple-monitors to forecast which country would come up a winner? As CFAs claim they can do via Pacioli's triple-monitors?

Um, probably not. I hope you begin to see that, just like Pacioli (and Tolstoy's Kutuzov), Marx also doesn't think people matter much. He only deals with inanimate stuff for his historical forecast. Money, land, labor in general. No Steve Jobses or Lee Iacoccas exist for him, just as they don't exist for Pacioli.

MARX: OWNERS WILL LOSE

Besides, and worse, Marx doesn't even perform a forecast. He just declares in advance that the end is inevitable: The workers will win, the owners will lose. Historical inevitability, he calls it.

One of these losing owners, by the way, is you. A stock owner. So no, Marx doesn't think much of you (or me, for that matter). He sees us as leeches on the backs of the workers.

But can his method of forecasting still work? Can a country be represented in a sort of Value Line one-pager? Like a stock? With its three kinds of resources? Land, capital, and labor? And if so, could its individual economic success be forecast via a Marxist methodology?

It might, or it might not. But would it help you forecast whether it'd win or lose a *war*?

Most likely not. As noted above, according to Marx *all* countries will lose eventually, and their owners (like you and me) be thrown on the ash heap of history. Then all countries will merge into one big communist kumbaya, where you and I will own nothing, and be happy, or else.

Obviously, Marxian analysis won't help you much in your quest as a BND analyst to forecast the result of the R – U war nor, as a stock analyst, to find out which stock would win, PEP or KO.

So what now?

Is there any other historian on your bookshelf who could forecast which country would win a battle? Whose method you'd try to apply to corporate market-share battles also?

Well, here is another historian, Oswald Spengler.

SPENGLER: THE WEST WILL DECLINE

Spengler wrote a few books that forecast the decline of the West. For him, like Marx, the end result was a forgone conclusion. The important factors, though, were different. Not exploitation and historical inevitability, but more like moral turpitude, loss of vigor, and retreat before hardier, more manly (his words) races.

However, again it's inevitable, a la Spengler, and therefore, like Pacioli's and Marx's methods, it's one where individual humans don't matter.

Who else do we have, then, among historians, who can forecast?

KONDRATIEF: IT'S UP AND DOWN, ENDLESSLY

Well, there's Nikolai Kondratief, both a historian and an economist, who one hundred years ago stated that business and the economy move in big, fifty-year cycles. Or was it sixty? Something like that. And within these large cycles there are mini cycles, and within these, smaller cycles still, and so on.

Yet when you get down to details, it doesn't work, because it's hard to know when a cycle (or a mini cycle) begins and another ends, until the cycle has ended, when it all becomes clear, and useless.

So Kondratief is out too.

MOMMSEN AND GIBBON: JUST MORE TRENDIES

Who else do we have?

Well, there's Mommsen and Gibbon, both of whom wrote beautifully about the decline of the Roman Empire, with the first also getting the Nobel Prize for the work, viewed as Literature (i.e., fiction. The other historian who got the Nobel for his work was Churchill. Yes, in the Literature category also.) However, both also say it was inevitable, and so they aren't good as forecasters either. Yes, they do mention some individual leaders who slowed down the decline, i.e., Iacoccas are possible but negligible), however their overall trend is down, and inevitable.

Who else is there, to help us forecast?

EARLY HISTORIANS COULD FORECAST BETTER

Let's go further back in time. And once we go back far enough, we see that Greek and Roman historians indeed saw individual leaders as important, some perhaps as all-important.

These earliest historians, like Thucydides and Herodotus and Plutarch (especially him), and later Titus Livius (see Machiavelli's book about him) frankly admitted that some men (and occasionally women) are vastly superior to others, and so can greatly influence events, while other people who are ordinary cannot, unless it is by accident.

Something like Pacioli's and Machiavelli's division of humanity into principals and agents, 2,000 years later, but explicitly so.

In simple words, for these early historians, leaders definitely make history, and so, when these early historians wrote history, it was mainly history of great men, i.e., biographies.

Let's take Plutarch, who wrote a magnificent two-volume set of biographies, aptly titled *Parallel Lives of the Noble Greeks and Romans*. In it, he paired each great Greek leader with his Roman parallel, based on common tasks, similar personal characteristics, or occasionally similar successes or misfortunes. For instance, city or nation builders, law-givers, wily strategists, etc.

In my strong opinion, every sleuth investor should read Plutarch twice over, then read him again if the sleuth has a particularly hard time identifying a leader's personality, or matching a CEO's personality to a situation. It is then useful to ask yourself: Which ancient leader does this CEO resemble? Because in some cases, the right kind of leader can change everything.

Yes, the direction of change is not certain, because history rarely repeats exactly. But it is said to occasionally rhyme, so such parallels are worthwhile for giving you an inkling about the future.

THE SCORE CARD OF GREAT SOULS

For example, Themistocles who, in Salamis, against all odds ensured that Europe stayed European and free, instead of turning Persian and enslaved. Or Lysander the Spartan, who conquered Athens with a trick more often seen in the boxing ring (called the "metronome," if you want to know). Or Coriolanus, a genius general who, by switching allegiance to another city, could bring victory with him with a near certainty. Something like Iacocca, who left Ford and went over to Chrysler. Or, like Mike Hurd, HP's CEO who was fired (most probably unjustly), and then crossed over to Oracle and gleefully beat HP in the market.

OR MAYBE A HINT ABOUT THE R - U WAR'S OUTCOME?

But oddly, you can also meet in ancient history one Agathocles, king of Sicily, whose name is today synonymous with an evil dictator who nevertheless was highly successful, because he acted ruthlessly, as Machiavelli recommended a millennium later, and did all the bad stuff at once, then let his people settle and enjoy a respite.

Yes, go read about old Agathocles, then see if he doesn't remind you of Russonia's leader. A little. Or maybe a lot? And if this is so, which ancient leader does Ukronia's leader bring to mind, and why? (Hint: a certain laconic Spartan.) And what relevance would this similarity bring to the question of the R vs. U war, and its ultimate winner? And how can this little exercise help you in the future to sleuth a company? It doesn't have to be a lot of help. Even a little can tip the balance, in your long-term contest with stay-at-home Internet clickers.

All of which is to say that, as a sleuth who aims to analyze corporate leaders so as to better forecast their corporate performance, and their stocks', you'd better bone up on history and ancient leaders' biographies, in order to *understand what makes exceptional people tick.*

NOT MANY EXCEPTIONAL PEOPLE IN DAILY LIFE

Such understanding cannot be gotten from numbers, you know, only via experience. But where can you get it? You surely can't meet in the normal course of your life many exceptional people—those with extraordinary vision and exceptional drive—so you'd better go where they are: in history.

It is perhaps an inefficient way of becoming a better sleuth, but nevertheless it is an *effective* one. And as every sleuth knows, effectiveness trumps efficiency every time. Doing the right thing at 80% efficiency trumps doing the wrong thing with 98% efficiency.

Yes, like using "System 1" thinking vs. using "System 2."

But how to do that in real life?

Assume you must gauge XYZ's CEO's character quickly. Can you?

The answer is that you can, if you have a *specific character trait* in mind for which to test. But can people be assessed directly? And if so, how?

PERSONAL INFORMATION IS OFTEN KEY

The answer is: by watching their *personal* behavior when they must make a decision.

It is well known that such personal info about foreign leaders is meticulously collected by intelligence services, to help estimate their future reactions.

Here are two cases of actual tests, one by an American opponent who tested an American leader, and the results this apparently led to, and another of how a foreign leader uses personal sleuthing as part of his modus operandi. Finally, there's also a case of sleuthing the character of a CEO, whose decision whether or not to raise a takeover bid mattered most to the sleuth investor.

This last case will be deemed fictional.

CASE 1. JFK SAVAGED BY KHRUSHCHEV—LEADING TO THE CUBAN MISSILE CRISIS

In June 1961, 44-year-old JFK, then US President for less than five months, was to meet Soviet Premier Nikita Khrushchev (NK), in Vienna.

The CIA had told JFK that Khrushchev viewed him as a weak leader, because he'd botched the Cuban Bay of Pigs invasion. The Soviet leader also saw JFK as a rich, immature boy, whose father, Joseph Kennedy (allegedly the former treasurer of the mob during prohibition), bought JFK the presidency. This the CIA didn't tell JFK, but we can read it in the KGB files, after the Soviet Union finally fell, inevitably.

Coming after Eisenhower, whom Khrushchev saw as a strong man of vision (same sources), JFK struck the Soviet as a weakling, and so he set out to test him, to make sure, before he (NK) planned future actions.

One of JFK's most trusted advisers, Averell Harriman, later told how he had travelled half the globe to have five minutes with JFK and warn him of the importance of not failing this head-to-head test with the Soviet premier.

JFK laughed it off— but then failed the test, badly.

In that meeting, JFK foolishly debated Khrushchev on Soviet economics, about which he knew little, then carelessly said he saw the Soviet Union as an equal, which reportedly threw the Soviet Premier into ecstasies, as he concluded he had a weak opponent whom he could best in future.

"He savaged me," Kennedy ruefully confessed afterwards.

That conclusion had real-world consequences.

First, the Soviets took a harsh line in East Berlin, where later they were to build a wall. JFK then had to send VP Johnson to Berlin with military troops, to show that the Americans were serious about defending it. However, it was a rearguard action shoring up that first bad impression, and it was not the end of the consequences. Soon came the Cuban Missile crisis, where Khrushchev sent nukes to the island facing Florida, and JFK had to stare the Soviet Navy down, risking a nuclear exchange—all because he had left his opponent with the wrong impression on that very first meeting.

Clearly, Khrushchev was testing JFK. Luckily JFK recovered, and within a few years, it was Khrushchev (who had come to the wrong conclusion) who was gone, now accused by his Kremlin colleagues of being an "Adventurist," i.e., a risk taker who'd lost a bet.

Are such tests of leaders happening today, too?

Almost every day.

Here is another, where the test was public, and seemingly minor.

CASE 2. PRESIDENT PUTIN SLEUTHING FOREIGN LEADERS

Two years before Covid, an Israeli delegation flew to Moscow to meet with President Vladimir Putin. It was a large delegation of several dozen. Ministers, assistant ministers, wives, commercial hopefuls, some semi-retired hush-hush functionaries now in biz, and security people. Some Israeli ministers had Russian background and spoke Russian fluently, so it was a boisterous, semi-friendly occasion.

Putin gave a speech, and everyone listened, rapt. (He's a good speaker.) At the end of the speech, cheekier visitors asked if they could take a selfie with him. Good-naturedly, Putin consented, dismissed his security people, and everyone snapped away on their cells.

WHO INITIATES, AND WHO RESPONDS

But as the wife of an important Israeli minister was snapping pics, Putin asked her husband: Who to whom?

What? asked the confused minister.

Oh, Putin explained, when I was speaking, I saw you and your wife holding hands. Who gave a hand to whom?

The minister was flabbergasted. Here was the head of a big power, who had just given an important speech to important visitors. But in the middle of the speech, he could glimpse personal details like that one, then ask about them—presumably to make the visitor feel good.

That tidbit appeared in the Israeli press, and so I asked a buddy (who is connected) about it.

Oh no, he said. Putin didn't ask this to make nice. He asked because *he really wanted to know.*

But why would he need to? I asked.

Because, said my friend, as a former KGB agent Putin always wants to know who holds personal authority, who's the one who sucks up. Who is the one who initiates, who the one that responds, so that in future negotiations, or even just future meetings with this minister, any little thing like that can give Putin an advantage, if he only pressed a little harder and acted bossy.

You're joking, I said.

No, said my buddy. I am not.

Was my buddy right? I don't know. I am just reporting it.

But how does all this help you sleuth better?

Here then, finally, is a case where the sleuth initiates the testing, for commercial purposes.

As said before, this one should be considered fictional.

CASE 3. WILL AN ACQUIROR RAISE ITS TAKEOVER BID?

Assume you have a position in Stock XY. You had bought it a few years back, and it has risen nicely. One day you come to the office and see the stock is up 15%—a small conglomerate had made a takeover bid for it at a premium. Let's call the Small Conglomerate SC.

Company XY is resisting the takeover. The stock is worth more, says its CEO (as he should). SC should raise its bid, or we'll look for other potential buyers.

As an XY owner, the questions before you are:

(1) Should you sell *some* XY now? Or (2) Sell the *entire* position? Or (3) Keep it all, and *hope* for (3.1) another bidder, or (3.2) a higher bid from SC?

You are fairly sure the stock is worth more, but not much more (although in a year or two it might be), so you're tempted to sell into the market (option 1). The only thing keeping you from doing so is *the possibility SC will raise its bid.*

What are the chances of that?

HOW TO GO ABOUT FINDING OUT?

If you are a CFA-type investor, you prowl through XY's financials on the Internet, compare these to other such companies, trying to see if Price to BV or Price to Sales, or other such criteria, indicate under- or over-valuation.

In other words, you stay in the domain of numbers and second-hand information that CFAs swim in, i.e., in the domain of symbols and fiction.

But how would you answer the question as a sleuth? (Do remember: the situation is fictional.)

SLEUTHING AN ACQUIROR'S CEO

To sleuth the character of anyone, you'd better meet him or her, to gauge it for yourself. This assumes (1) you can meet, and (2) have experience in forming such judgements. Later we'll see how you can increase your expertise in such matters, but in this fictional case, your need is immediate—the takeover is ongoing—and your chances of meeting the CEO are zip.

What can you do, then?

The only thing you can do is *ask others for their opinion.*

But which others? How to find them? And what would you ask them about?

Luckily, the only question you have is: how likely is this CEO to overbid. In other words: How careful and stingy is he in matters of money, or, alternately, how careless and large? Every little bit of real info in that regard can give you an edge over CFA types who only watch the screen.

But how to do this?

CREATIVITY AND DARING GIVE A SLEUTH AN EDGE

This is where creativity and inventiveness help. First, you look up the address of SC's corporate headquarters. It's in a medium-sized town on the US East coast. Next, you close your office, put on your travel shoes, and fly there. You lodge in a hotel nearby and go see SC's HQ. It is situated in a small plaza furnished with all the amenities capitalism can provide. Mall, supermarkets, a bowling alley, a gym, several bank branches, ice cream parlor.

And there are also some restaurants. You visit a few and engage the staff with small talk, especially about their august local corporate resident. Do the executives eat in this restaurant?

The answer you get is that the lower staff eat at Subway, the execs eat Italian, but the highest bosses eat in the fake French Bistro, which we'll call Fancy Eats (FE).

So you tighten your tie and go eat at FE also, and as you order Surf and Turf (it comes under a French name), you chat with the server, a handsome woman in her late thirties. Yes, she says, Mr. Big and his team eat here. They like it, especially what you ordered.

QUESTIONING A POTENTIAL INFORMER

Ah, you say. And are they big tippers?

This, of course, is your main question, so you don't jump into it. Rather you gently lead into it.

However, by and by, you do learn that the tip depends.

Depends on what? you ask.

Well, says the server (whom you had tipped liberally the day before), it depends on whether he eats with his wife, or with his VPs.

Oh? You say. Depends how?

Well, says the server, if he's with the wife—his third by the way—he is a 10 percenter. But when he is with his boys, it's 25 or 30 percent, on the company's black Amex card.

You both have a laugh, as you note the fact down in your sleuth's brain. The trip, you conclude, has probably been worth it. Because the anecdote as much as proves that while Mr. Big is stingy with his own money, he is quite careless with the company's funds. So, the possibility he would raise his bid is suddenly looking more likely.

But just to make conversation, you also say, so all servers must compete to serve Mr. Big when he comes with the VPs, no?

Oh, no, says the server, with a grimace, and adds that Mr. Big has what was formerly known as Long Hands, and what today would be known as a #MeToo problem.

Ah, you say, nod sympathetically, and go to your food. Then you tip medium-liberally (so as not to leave too big an impression), and leave.

RE-ASSIGNING THE SLEUTHING JOB

You don't go back to FE, but instead call your office, and have your assistant take the next plane there. She arrives, and goes to FE for lunch. Your assistant is a pleasant, competent middle-aged woman with an MBA and black belt in kung fu. She chats with the server, as woman to woman, and eventually learns that although Mr. Big pays handsomely, servers don't want to serve his table. It is not worth the aggravation.

But, your assistant then adds, girl to girl, if he's married a third time, perhaps a lucky server can stretch her luck and become Mrs. Big #4?

It is then that she hits even bigger paydirt. Because what she learns is that Mr. Big has had #MeToo problems for several years, so three secretaries at SC quit and sued, and the board, which values Mr. Big's management skills, bought off their complaints. This, says the server, is well known. But it is also rumored he was given an ultimatum that if there's a fourth, he's gone.

And? your assistant says. So he's good now?

No, your assistant learns. There *was* a fourth case. So Mr. Big, desperate, promised to divorce wife #3 and marry the secretary, which he did—it cost him fifty mil—but it didn't help. His days are numbered.

Well, well, murmurs your assistant, and soon reports to you.

This is what's called a sleuth's serendipity.

LADY LUCK SMILES ON YOU

You had looked for info about the chances of overpaying for the takeover (the CEO did, by the way, so you sold half the position at the market, then sold the other half a dollar fifty higher), but then inadvertently learned something much more valuable—that Mr. Big's days were numbered.

Is Wall Street aware of it?

You check with your broker's analyst, and realize that some indeed are, but are discreetly quiet. Because this does not relate to the stock, after all.

Or does it?

Apparently it does. Because SC Inc. has all sorts of Special Purpose financial vehicles offshore, only partly revealed in footnotes, of which the CFO is not officially aware—as is apparent from corporate earnings calls, to which you re-listen.

So, the question becomes: If Mr. Big goes, who'd be the next CEO?

Wall Street is sure it is the EVP/COO. However, because of the #MeToo issues, the CFO (whose secretary became Mrs. Big #4) has a great card to play. If he (the CFO) doesn't get the job, then the *New York*

Times and/or *The Washington Post* would likely get an anonymous tip about the #MeToo problem.

And that's why, when Mr. Big soon leaves, the CFO becomes the new CEO, to Wall Street's surprise, and it then takes him three years to learn of (and resolve) the offshore problems, which are bigger than anyone had expected.

SC STOCK SINKS AS NEW CEO DISCOVERS TRUE PROBLEMS

And during those three years, SC's stock steadily sinks 60% as write-offs accumulate, and the dividend is cut, then cut again, so those who had shorted it make good money.

Of course, as I said, it's a fictional tale, but it gives you a clue about how to get information in case you need it. There are always sources, and it's up to you to recruit them. Or, if such is not in your skill set, hire those who can, and let them do it, and pay them.

All of which is to say that leadership does matter—not only its talents, but also its flaws. Both in politics, and in the market.

But how to gauge such flaws? And how to find them?

We'll find out in the next chapter.

SUMMARY IMPLICATIONS FOR YOUR INVESTMENTS:

- **Resist the rush to find answers on the Internet** just because it's convenient.
- **Look for *human* sources who can answer your question,** legally and ethically.
- ***Recruit* them yourself** if you can, **or *delegate*** the task to others if you cannot.
- **Keep yourself *open*** to answers to questions you didn't even have.
- **Keep your mouth shut** when/if you get the answer(s).

CHAPTER 3
GENERALS' POINT OF VIEW

Sleuthing CEOs. Boney vs. Nosey, and the near-run-thing.

How much do leaders' flaws matter?

Let's go back to Napoleon, whom we've left retreating from Moscow, which he shouldn't have attacked in the first place.

Since his 1812 retreat, Napoleon had managed to lose a battle in Leipzig, then be captured in Paris by the European powers, and in 1814, be exiled to the island of Elba.

However, less than a year later, in March 1815, Napoleon managed to escape, returned to France, recaptured the hearts of many, and planned to continue where he had left off.

By June 1815, however, Napoleon was again facing the combined forces of Britain, Prussia, Austria, the Low Lands and some Irish and Scottish, all aiming to stop him for good.

As this sleuthing tutorial begins, Napoleon faces the battle of Waterloo.

BONEY AND NOSEY, AND FIELD MARSHAL FORWARD

The Prussians are led by Field Marshal Blucher, then 82 years young, nicknamed Field Marshal Forward by his troops, who dote on him because he participated in all their chores. Remember their fondness to him. It is part of this tutorial.

The Alliance's forces are led by General Arthur Wellesley, aka Lord Wellington, for whom soldiers have high respect, though not exactly love. (He used to hang or flog miscreants.) Wellington's nickname was Nosey, because of his long aristocratic nose. So perhaps it does show some irreverent fondness. You decide.

Napoleon's nickname, on the other hand, (among the Brits), was Boney, short for Bonaparte. As for the French troops: Napoleon's soldiers had no nickname for him, but admired him profusely and risked their lives just to get a pinch on the cheek (or by the ear) from him, which was his rare mark of affection.

HOW FAR WOULD RANK AND FILE GO, FOR THE CHIEF?

Much later (I'm jumping the gun here), Apple's employees would postpone weddings to finish projects by Jobs' deadline. Even though, like Wellington's soldiers, Apple employees did not love Jobs. But as with Wellington, they respected Jobs greatly, because he expected a lot from them, had a vision, worked hard for it, and gave them leeway to make their decisions. And yes, they did have a nickname for Jobs: Elvis.

All the last are part of this tutorial also, examples of how the led see the leader.

As, by the way, is this:

BLIND OBEDIENCE VS. INITIATIVE

No French soldier or officer had the freedom to override Napoleon's command, certainly not to the extent that Wellington allowed his troops. Napoleon was the single Decider. What's even more interesting, from letters and dispatches, is that Wellington often chose his officers and noncoms (i.e., sergeants and such) partly for their risk taking, i.e., not just risking their lives, but also risking his displeasure if they acted on what was right for the situation, even if his orders were otherwise.

Napoleon, on the other hand, chose his commanders because of their loyalty and near-blind obedience. He needed this because he thought he was a genius, so his plan was impeccable and not to be messed with.

Remember this part too.

Now back to Waterloo, where the future of Europe is about to be determined, and history is being written. Whose view do you think would prove correct here, Tolstoy's, or Dostoevsky's? Were Nosey and Boney (and F.M. Forward) writing it? Or were they merely history's quills?

We shall soon see.

Before the battle, Wellington had agreed that he (plus the Irish and Scottish and Dutch) would fight and hold off the French, but he needed the Prussians to come help him in time, to finish it. Napoleon guessed that this was part of Wellington's plan, and so, on the day before the battle, August 17, he sent about a fifth of his force to hunt the Prussian forces who'd escaped after the Battle of Ligny (which the Prussians had lost), and were now making their way to Waterloo.

NAPOLEON CHOOSES A GENERAL

Napoleon thought he knew which way the Prussians would take, so that's where he sent his force to hold them off. This holding-off was a crucial task, so the question before Napoleon was: Who to appoint as commander of this critical stopping-job?

Here, then, is where the actual sleuthing tutorial begins:

Napoleon chose General Emmanuel de Grouchy, a loyal acolyte of his, to lead the Prussian stopping force. And in this choice, Napoleon likely lost the battle of Waterloo, as well as his army and his empire. Another result of this far-off choice is that this book is now written in English, not in French. But that's just by the by.

Now let me be clear: Grouchy was not a bad general. He was also not a bad man. He came from a distinguished family full of liberal ideas, and his sister, Sophie Grouchy, had married the Marquis de Condorcet, who was the first to agitate for women's voting rights, and wrote a famous pamphlet about it.

A GOOD GENERAL BUT ALSO A YES-MAN

So, a conformist Grouchy was not. But he was still a yes-man. And because he was so obedient, *he followed Napoleon's order to the letter and attacked the Prussians where Napoleon said they would be.* But unbeknownst to Grouchy (and Napoleon), the force he was attacking was just the rearguard of the Prussian army, that is, the tail end. The main body was already halfway down to the battlefield, with their cannons. In fact, Grouchy could hear some Prussian cannons firing on his left, not on the right, but *he dared not change his orders,* and so he kept after the Prussians' tail, and received universal opprobrium for it ever after.

Which, in my opinion, was not fully deserved, since it was Napoleon's choice to put Grouchy there, because Napoleon thought himself a total genius and so required total obedience, i.e., Grouchy's. And because of that, Napoleon lost at Waterloo and we all speak English.

NAPOLEON'S CHARACTER WEAKNESS—CONCEIT—LOST HIM HIS KEY BATTLE

So, at least in this sleuth's interpretation, *it was Napoleon's character that lost him the battle.* His choice of Grouchy was really a function of Napoleon's own character. *He chose Grouchy because Grouchy was an obedient* yes-man, which is what conceited ego-driven geniuses require.

Of course, this was not the only reason Napoleon lost. The other two reasons were Blucher's and Wellington's characters.

OPPONENTS' CHARACTERS ARE IMPORTANT, TOO

First, wily Field Marshal Blucher realized early that Napoleon would be sending a force to forestall him. So instead of going straight in, he circled around, to avoid them, ordering his loyal troops to drag their cannons through the mud for the entire night, in a hellish rain storm. When the troops began to slow down, Blucher rode up and down their lines, admonishing them that he had given his word of honor to Lord Wellington that they'd be there on time. Would they now make him break his word?

And because Blucher's soldiers loved him, they doubled their efforts, and made it on time.

That was one reason.

The second reason was that the Prussian soldiers also esteemed Lord Wellington, and did not want their general to lose face with him, nor did they want to be the reason for it. So not only Napoleon's character played a part in his loss, but so did Blucher's and so did Wellington's.

Yet if you want to narrow Napoleon's loss to one reason, it was most likely that he had chosen his generals for blind loyalty and blind obedience, because of overweening confidence in his own perfect ability.

Thus on June 18, 1815, when Grouchy should have headed towards the Prussian cannons, he still decided to stick to his orders, and so brought the Alliance its victory, which nevertheless was, in Wellington's own words, a "damn near-run thing."

FOOTBALL VS. BASKETBALL COACHES

Switching for a moment from war and finance to a sports analogy, Napoleon behaved like an American football coach, whose players often have earphones under their helmets, and so can obey detailed orders by the coach, like toy robots, during the entire game. Wellington, on the other hand, behaved like a basketball coach who explains the game to his players in advance, trains them in the main combinations, but then must trust them to make up their mind on the fly during the game. For example, when to take a chance on a risky triple-pointer, when to hand the ball to a team mate, when to foul for strategic reasons, or when to wait till the last second to take a shot.

Character matters, both in war and in sports—and in the market.

To conclude, then: Does Dostoevsky's viewpoint win here, finally? Is that the kind of CEO you want running the companies behind your stocks?

Not so fast. It is not that simple.

It is easy to say you should always look for a Wellington, who knows how to operate with partners, gives his people leeway, and so wins both the battle and his people's esteem, and that you should avoid hard-ass egotistical geniuses like Napoleon who hire yes-people only.

THERE'S A TIME AND PLACE FOR BOTH A NOSEY AND A BONEY

However, the real answer is: *it depends on the situation.*

You must remember that in *some* situations a Napoleon *is* called for. For example, in turnarounds, or in ongoing disasters that must be forestalled, where fast decisions must be made on the fly, without debate. Thus, when a corporate CEO is trying to avert clear disaster, a good rule is to siphon all decision-making into his or her hands, no second guessing, and allow more down-stream initiative only once the situation has stabilized.

But in regular, stable situations, where there's time for planning, then taking initiative close to the customer is where extra profit and corporate goodwill usually lie. There, CEOs who hire for blind obedience are likely to cost you, the shareholder, money.

So when should you look for which type? How to know whether the CEO's character fits the corporate situation? Are there any other rules?

The answer is: not always, and *it is up to you to decide what kind of situation the company is in, and whether the CEO's character suits the situation.*

To learn how to discern this takes experience. But there are a number of books about past leaders of both types, the problems they tackled, and why they succeeded or failed.

And yes, most of these books are history books, and mostly very old. Like the historians mentioned in the previous chapter. See the additional list at the end of this book.

However, just to make it clearer, let's relate two concrete examples that show, first, the risk hiding in a character flaw of an otherwise superlative manager, and second, the opposite: the advantage hiding in the character of another such master, who is more of an investor than a manager.

First is a personality risk hiding in plain sight:

A. STEVE JOBS AND THE HIRING OF PEPSI'S CEO

In 1983, as its home computer caught on, Apple entered a rapid growth mode, and its CEO, Steve Jobs, realized he needed a professional CEO to run the company, so he, Jobs, could focus on the innovation side.

When Jobs tried to convince the young CEO of Pepsi Cola to leave Pepsi and become Apple's CEO, the young CEO—let's call him Sam here—kept resisting. To break Sam's resistance, Jobs finally told him the following: "Do you want to spend the rest of your life selling colored fizzy water to children, or do you want to help change the world?" And although Sam was older than Jobs, and more experienced, he caved in and joined Apple.

Why did Sam cave in?

Because Jobs, who was a Principal with a strong vision of his own, realized that Sam was an agent in his soul. (See again for the definition, in Chapter 1.) So Jobs touched by instinct on the sorest point of all agents: they strive to get someone *else*'s respect and approval. Whose? If we could peek into Sam's heart, we may find some former school teacher he was trying to impress, because he had told the young Sam he wouldn't amount to much; or maybe an elder brother whom his parents had loved more; or perhaps a distant father, or maybe the entrepreneur who had started Pepsi, or perhaps, oddly, the CEO of Coke, his main competitor, who'd nod approvingly and say, Well done, Sam. Good boy!

In other words: although Sam was clearly a leader, his soul was one of an agent who serves the vision of *others*. Jobs instantly saw this, identifying Sam as someone craving acceptance and respect—which is the one thing Jobs denied him, unless he joined Apple.

Jobs, by the way, apparently had no such person he was trying to impress. It appears he was only trying to impress himself by fulfilling his own vision. But that's just by the by.

Sam might, of course, have said: Making a few more millions a year (and having the key to the CEO's washroom of a Fortune 500 company) is more important to me than changing the world. Or, he may have responded with: Selling home computers will not change the world. The first answer would tag him as a crass and inferior human being. The second would have landed him right into Jobs' argument, because Jobs could then launch into his pitch of how home computers *would* change the world. (As indeed they have.)

Sounds clever and nifty?

THE TWIN DOWNSIDES OF SUCH AN ARGUMENT

Well, yes. But there are two bad costs to the above method as used by Jobs, both stemming from Jobs' character flaw:

1. *First cost: it is immoral*

Jobs' argument was surely effective; but it was also insidious, and thus *immoral.* Because when Jobs denigrated Sam's entire career with a single poisoned question, he effectively said: Your entire life has been contemptible, so your entire achievement—becoming a CEO, being rich, serving as director of several companies, does not impress me in the least, since essentially all you are is a fancy sugar-water salesman—and for children to boot. So (and this was implied), you don't have *my* respect. If you want it, come help *me* change the world, under *my* vision, and then maybe I'll respect you.

Of course you might ask: How did Jobs become the person whose respect and esteem were worth having more than those of others? Part of this was due to the strength of his vision, and part due to his monomaniacal focus on it. His total lack of scruples of how to achieve his vision is the flaw that this tutorial aims to highlight.

2. *Second cost: Jobs' poisoned question would boomerang onto Jobs himself*

Yet Jobs succeeded: in that one deadly phrase, he peeled it all away from Sam, and yes, he got Sam to join. But the cost to Jobs—and to his shareholders—would be high, although it was in the far future, and neither he nor they knew it yet. Because from that moment on, it was likely that, after Sam had gotten Jobs' approval, he may try to get even—which is apparently what happened ten years later, when the board fired Jobs, which nearly ruined Apple in the process, driving the stock price to a shade above cash per share.

Any sleuth who had learned of Sam's hiring should have had some misgiving about the future relationship at the top of Apple, because of the risk that Jobs' character flaw had created. Lack of scruples nearly always does.

On the other hand:

With Sam gone (he failed of course, since he apparently had no vision of his own), Jobs was summoned back to Apple by the board. Anyone who'd bought the stock then (at a smidgen above cash per share), betting on Jobs' immoral genius, would have made a fortune.

The market is not a church, you know.

B. WARREN BUFFETT AND TOM SAWYER'S APPLE

Now to show you the other side, where a wily but honest character creates continuous future benefits, here is Warren Buffett's use of the opposite of what Jobs did.

An analyst once asked Buffett:

With the proliferation of private equity (that is: levered buyout) firms, what can Berkshire Hathaway (Buffett's company) offer to a proposed acquisition's owner, more than others can, besides a higher price? And won't this increasing competition detract from Berkshire's future prospects, because it would have to pay more for future companies it wants to buy?

Buffett's answer was:

We tell the owner, Yes you may sell your lovely company that it had taken you thirty years to build, for a bit more money from some other buyer, who'll give it a nose job and put big boobs on it, then put it in the sales window and peddle it to the first old man in a raincoat that comes along. Or, you can sell your beloved company to us, and we'll treat it with respect, then put it in the Berkshire museum for all future generations to behold and admire.

To read this is to marvel at Buffett's genius. It is close to Jobs' words to Sam, but without the poisonous edge. To the contrary: whereas Jobs denigrated Sam's past achievement, in order to convince him to join Apple, Buffett complimented the acquisition-target's owner on his achievement, then presented Berkshire's offer really *as a reward for excellence*, that would constitute an even higher achievement... Really the ultimate accolade in business. Like a Napoleon offering a cheek-pinch, or a medal...

Was there poison here? Not really, or rather, perhaps some: No matter what you, Mr. Owner, achieves, *it will never be recognized fully without Berkshire's imprimatur* of a Buyout offer.

So yes, leavened with humor, it does not denigrate the seller's lifework; "only" his desire to sell his innocent corporate daughter for "merely a bit more money…"

How's that for negotiating skills? It is really close to Tom Sawyer's achievement, when he convinced his buddies that it's not a chore to paint his aunt's fence, but an honor for which they should pay *him*, rather than the other way around.

Just see what low price Buffett paid for the Israeli machine-tool maker Iscar. The price he paid was extremely reasonable, as the owner himself later grudgingly admitted.

Alright, sleuthing for character does work, interrogating informers works, and you should do more of both.

But just *how* to do it, to get a leg up against stay-at-home (or the office) CFAs?

CHAPTER 4
INTEL OPERATIVES' POINT OF VIEW

Boffins vs. sleuths, and what SigInt misses.

In 1989, General Vernon Walters was the US ambassador to Germany, residing in the West Berlin embassy. At the time, Walters was a sixtyish, corpulent, jovial guy, whom State Dept opponents often described as garrulous—and he could be both, in six languages, which he spoke perfectly: both highbrow and the vernacular. French, German, Italian, Portuguese, Spanish, and of course English. His diplomatic career followed his elevation to #2 man of the CIA; and that was after a long and distinguished career in military intelligence and in the White House, where he was a high-level trouble shooter for three presidents.

Now why is all this relevant in a book about advanced sleuthing?

FORECASTING THE BERLIN WALL'S FALL

Because at the beginning of November 1989 (or so the apocryphal story goes), Ambassador Walters went for a morning stroll in East Berlin. (Other stories say it was in the evening.) He was followed by some sheepish East German spooks, as well as by embassy-CIA minders just in case, even though there was little physical danger to him: at the time, East and West spooks did not harm each other needlessly, unlike today.

But I digress.

As Ambassador Walters walked down blustery East Berlin streets (so goes the story), he chatted to the locals: taxi drivers, ladies of the night and their pimps (all of whom were part-time Stasi informers), biergarten waiters, layabouts and street cleaners (some of whom were full-time spooks), and occasional passersby. Speaking the Platt-Deutsch vernacular, he asked about their families, children, health, and their views of the world; and he listened. He also offered them American cigarettes, told off-color jokes and laughed at theirs; then he returned to the embassy. Once back he napped briefly, then sent his boss, US Secretary of State, whom I'll call Barkley, a coded diplomatic cable, saying East Berlin was about to blow in a week.

And now, a sidebar:

For the previous three years, Walters had forecast that Germany would very soon unify. This was contrary to both State Dept and CIA official views, and did not make him popular. But since the President held him in high esteem, he was tolerated.

This time, however, Walters also gave a date. And he put it in a cable. To the Sec of State Himself. Officially. As Martin Luther had put it in 1522, nailing his view to a church door not far away: That's how I stand.

Barkley called Walters immediately. (Or thus, at least, goes the story.)

Where the hell did you get this? Barkley asked, irate. None of our people heard anything, nor the CIA. Neither agents nor agent runners nor wire tappers. So, what the hell? Where is it from?

It's on the street, said Walters. Everyone feels it in their bones.

What bones? Like who, everyone?

Everyone: hookers, pimps, cab drivers, waiters, street cleaners, Stasi part-timers. They all feel something is up. In a week, they say, not longer.

Fiddlesticks, said Barkley (whose nickname was the Silken Mallet, of which he was proud and tried to live up to). We have agents everywhere. The mistress of Honecker (East Germany's Chief) is on our payroll. He's sick and we even know his medications. We know top local spooks in the Stasi, we bug half of them and pay the other half. And they listen to everyone's phone, and then we listen to them—and no one said a thing! Not one!

STANDING UP TO PRESSURE

I don't care, said Walters. A week, everyone says. At most. It's in my cable.

Claptrap, Barkley said. Withdraw the cable. I don't want Congress on my back for such unsubstantiated twaddle.

Nope. Walters said, I will not withdraw it. The cable stays, and by the way I have a copy, just in case. And also by the way, I too have friends in Congress.

Let's pause here for another side bar with a quote from an old Roman politician named Seneca, who said: All human virtues aren't worth crap without the most important of all: *Courage*.

Of which, evidently, Walters had lots—which, by the way, he had used several times before, first as Deputy Director of the CIA when President Nixon wanted the CIA to lie and save his (Nixon's) butt during Watergate, and Walters told him no. He even offered to resign if they pushed him. Just as (allegedly) he was offering to do now. And, he also stood up later to George Shultz, then Secretary of State (and also one of my Stanford GSB professors) who didn't like Walters' close friendship with Ronald Reagan.

Did I say cojones already?

But back to the Berlin story. The upshot was that General Walters' cable to Barkley stayed and today is on the record, probably somewhere in the CIA museum in Langley, VA. (The CIA gave Walters a medal for standing up to the White House in the Watergate case; the State Dept, where he stood up to Barkley, gave him nothing.)

Now why is the above notable?

SLEUTHED INFORMATION PROVES PRESCIENT

Because a week later, on the night between November 8 and 9, without any apparent pre-meditation, nearly everyone in East Berlin—who'd been under the Soviet boot for years—picked up shovels, axes, hammers, and as if sleepwalking, went on a rampage to destroy the Berlin Wall.

No pre-planning, they'd just had enough—and history changed on a pfennig.

By morning, East Berliners streamed to West Berlin freely, and next day East and West Berlin became one city. In a year, Germany itself became one country, and two years after the Wall fell, in 1991, the Soviet Union itself fell, as Gorbachev tried to fix the unfixable—none of which, of course, the CIA foresaw.

Only General Walters did, in the case of the Berlin Wall—and he did this by talking to people directly. The lowest kind of people, the common folks.

And what again does all this have to do with advanced sleuth investing?

Quite a lot, actually:

The Fall of the Berlin Wall was not foreseen by any of the professional spooks of the CIA. Neither agent runners, nor phone eavesdroppers, nor satellite image analyzers, nor code breakers, and certainly not the back-office PhDs in Sovietology. The sole person who not only foresaw it but also gave the exact timing was a jovial old guy who liked to chat with low-level people on the spot, spoke their language, and so got the truth they felt in their bones.

Chatting, listening—and no ink squiggles.

But *why* exactly did General VW succeed?

Because he went after information that no office-dwelling egghead had, and because he went after it *directly*. Not via ink or blips—that is, via analytical documents, whether unclassified or secret, with info obtained by *others*. Nor did he have any backchannels to the political underground, because there were none. One of the Stasi's Soviet overlords, one Vladimir Vladimirovich (nicknamed Vova) Putin, then stationed in East Berlin, saw to it.

So no, Walters used no spook stuff. He used direct senses, his own, like sight and sound and smell and touch, and most important, a feeling in his own ample gut about the gut views of people who lived the local reality day-by-day.

And he got all this by asking for their opinions.

Now, just to be perfectly frank:

PERSONAL MEETING HELPED

Vernon Walters had also met Gorbachev himself, and sat beside him and his wife Raisa at a dinner, so when he chatted to them, he also had the opportunity to gauge their views and personalities. Which not many in the State Dept had—although Barkley certainly had, and yet it did not help *him* form the right view, because he rarely listened to others' views. Vernon Walters did, so he concluded that in the coming, popular spontaneous uprising, Gorbachev would probably not unleash the Soviet army or the KGB, as the Soviet Union had done before, in Hungary and Czechoslovakia.

This was also the opinion of Raisa, Gorby's life partner, whose views Walters got by chatting to her at dinner. Barkley was there too, but he apparently listened to neither highly placed nor lowly folks whose views were contrary to his, and so history notes that he got it wrong, while Vernon Walters got it right.

And now, before you ask:

Why couldn't General Walters pass along his info to his boss, complete with details, so as to convince him?

INFORMATION CAN BE PASSED ALONG, BUT CONVICTION CANNOT

The answer is: he could pass along as many details as he wished. What he couldn't pass along was his *conviction* resulting from *his* interaction with the informers, which brought up *previous* interactions with *other* informers of his, that had coalesced to a certainty *then*, and so ensured that the recent interaction coalesce into a certainty *now*.

However, that certainty was for him alone.

In short, *it was "System 1" thinking which brought up* ***a conclusion that belonged exclusively to General Vernon Walters***, the same observer who had *created* that info together with his informers, during a temporary personal relationship. Any attempt to transfer this *total matrix* without all the background interactions, both internal and external, would've rendered it useless, because no listener could *feel* what GVW felt. *This personal feeling of his was part of the info matrix—indeed was the key to it,* as Walters' hippocampus went looking for that piece of Dark Information tucked away in Walters' own past feelings. That missing Dark Info was pure feeling wrapped in images and muscle memory as well as words and notes and a mish-mash of pre-categorized sensory info that had been stored there, *before* parts of it had been passed through his cortex which, together with his hippocampus, produced that now-famous forecast.

SIDE BAR: IMPLICATIONS FOR INVESTMENT MANAGEMENT OPERATIONS—AND FOR SLEUTHS

The above is the main reason why the traditional division of intelligence operations like the CIA and other bureaucratic intel services, do such a lousy forecasting job. That's because all such services are *split into four parts*: agents, agent runners, back-office analysts (aka boffins), and customers, aka trigger pullers.

As detailed in my first book, *TSI, this very same structure operates both on Wall Street and in large money-management companies.* They too have info sources, info source handlers, analysts, and portfolio managers/trigger pullers.

The first problem is that, just as in the CIA and its ilk, the first two functions are also deficient in Wall Street and money management firms. Practically no one talks to low-level sources, like machinists or engineers, and certainly no one sleuths physically outside the office (besides schmoozing clients). Everyone wants to do high-status, highly paid CFA analysis in an air-conditioned office, or be a trigger-puller/portfolio manager based on CFA's squiggly output.

SEPARATION OF FOUR INTEL PROFESSIONS: THE MAIN CULPRIT OF FORECAST FAILURE

But the second, and more severe, problem is that the very *separation* of the four jobs makes the resulting info weak and often useless, because only those who *created* it can have the *conviction* derived from handling non-categorized, physical information. Only when these four jobs merge in a single, talented sleuth can they create both original true *information* and personal *conviction* that leads to correct action—and so take CFAs' money.

Because Wall Street, the same as the CIA and its ilk, cannot mend its ways (*authority at the top has no true info + conviction, whilst true info + conviction at the bottom has no authority*), this naturally presents opportunities to sleuths, who do what these behemoths won't do. As did General Vernon Walters, who unified all the functions in himself (liberally basted with courage).

So, once again: What are the implications of the above for your own investing?

For this, let me segue to another true story, this one about IBM—and, yes, again, Warren Buffett.

WARREN AND CHARLIE BUY INTO IBM

In 2011, Buffett made an investment in IBM—a very large one: $10.7 billion: 64 million shares at $176 per share. And this, please note, was after repeatedly denying he would invest in technology, since he didn't understand it. Still, it was Warren Buffet, so because I had once run a top-performing value tech fund, friends and old partners asked me what I thought of the IBM purchase. Should one follow on Buffett's coattails? Surely Warren and Charlie had spoken to IBM's top people and done their due diligence?

This must have been so. However, since I never invest based on others' work, I decided to sleuth it too.

How?

I asked techie friends if they knew anyone who worked for IBM—low- and mid-level only. Not VPs, not officers of the company, not top dogs, just common workers. Only corporals, sergeants and lieutenants, so to speak, not generals or even colonels.

After a while, I got a few names plus permission to mention my introducer so I could be checked out, and I began calling. Some contacts I met in person, over a beer or coffee, and I asked questions.

And now another sidebar:

PERSONAL INTRODUCTIONS TAKE TIME—BUT ARE CRUCIAL

Unless you are an experienced sleuth and know how to make strangers talk, do not try to bypass the introduction stage. It may take you a few weeks more, but it's worth it. Because if you call and say, "Hi, you don't know me, but I run money and I wonder if you can tell me…" it's very different from calling and saying, "Mr. Jones? Tim Jones? Hi. My name is Joe Barr. Your friend Sammy Finkel gave me your name, and said you might be able to help me."

Different, isn't it?

In a way, sleuthing via referrals is like looking for a job. Your time is best spent getting an introduction to a person inside the company, by someone who knows people in the company you are interested in—and who can vouchsafe for you. And it should be someone who agrees to confirm the reference if the person you are calling then calls him or her and asks who you are.

It's like the difference between a guy calling a girl and saying, Hi, my name is Sam, you don't know me, but I wonder if... Or, on the other hand, saying, Hi, is it Laurette? I met your cousin Gloria in the church Dance for Charity on Sunday, and she said I should give you a call, because we both have an interest in pure-breed Spaniels. Do you?

See?

Anyway, the people in IBM I was introduced to were both engineers and sales people. And since I was once an engineer too, I could speak to them both in English and Technicalese, and so could strike a rapport—especially since I came recommended. And even more especially, since I listened, and because I asked for their *personal* opinions.

NO CONTACT WITH COMPANY OFFICERS

To be sure, I also knew a divisional controller at IBM, a Stanford GSB grad, but avoided calling her, because she was an officer of the company, and I didn't want to talk to anyone who could give me privileged information, which would put both of us in hot water.

Remember, I only wanted personal opinions.

So how did the conversations go?

After mentioning that I'd been given their names by a mutual friend, I presented myself and said I was with a money-management firm running both private money and pension funds. Promising confidentiality, I then asked a few simple questions:

- What exactly do you do at IBM? How did you get to do it? (Here the person started talking about him/herself. This is always a favorite subject for the talker.)

- How do you like it? Do you like your job? If so, why? If not, why not?
- How do you like your boss or bosses? If so, why? If not, why not?
- What do you think they are doing right, or wrong? Nothing confidential, just in general.
- If the latter, did you tell them? Can you tell them?
- What do you think your bosses think of their boss? Can they tell him or her?
- And finally, about the company's CEO: What do you think of her? Do you understand her strategy? If you were in her place, *what would you do differently*?

BEST SLEUTHING TOOL: YOUR EARS

Then I let them speak, and listened. As you can see, the questions start from the bland and innocuous, then become more specific and pointed. And of course, if at any point you feel that the person is reluctant to talk, just thank them, ask if they can refer you to someone else in the company (at this point they often refuse), and go on to the next contact.

And of course, take notes. No, no recordings. Never. Just notes.

Now, you may well ask, why would they speak to me?

The answer is, *Because I asked for their opinions*. It's as simple as that. In the corporate world, it's not very common for low-level or mid-level workers to be asked for their honest opinions. So if you do, and you are genuinely interested, you'd be astonished at how hungry most are for having their opinions solicited.

But, you may still ask, how valuable is what they have to say? After all, they are just low-level cogs in the machine, are they not? How much do they really understand?

DISMISSIVE ATTITUDE RUINS COMPANIES—AND SLEUTHING

Excuse me for saying this, but it's this dismissive attitude that often wrecks companies—but luckily, its opposite usually makes them flourish. And of course, it helps make sleuths flourish—so long as they stay away from talking to officers of the company.

MACHINIST THE SMARTEST PERSON AT DANA CORP

Rene McPherson, the former chairman of Dana Corporation, a car-parts supplier, became briefly the dean of the Stanford Graduate School of Business, my alma mater. It was a brief tenure, unfortunately, because he was hit by a car after his nomination and passed away soon after. But he said a lot of wise things while he was in the role, and one saying in particular struck me the most, in response to a question he was asked by a student: Who was the smartest manager in your company?

McPherson said it was not the CFO, nor any of the VPs, all of whom were very smart—certainly smarter than me (he said). Rather, it was the machinist who worked the lathe on the shop floor.

How come? asked the student.

Because, said Rene McPherson, that guy (in those years it was only a guy) made 15 grand a year plus a bonus of 3 (this of course was in the pre-history), but on this salary, he raised a family, paid the mortgage, saved for college for his kids, bought his wife a dress for Xmas and put aside some money for a new fishing pole.

That machinist, said McPherson, was the smartest manager in Dana Corp. So if I, the CEO, didn't make a point to ask him what he thought about the company, what was right and what was wrong in the corporate plan, and what should be done to make it better, then both the company and I, its CEO, were missing a lot.

This answer left a big impression on me, and ever since, I have made a point to ask low- and mid-level employees what they thought of their company's strategy, what they would do better, and why. Then I shut up and listen. And ever since I've been constantly surprised by their insights, how much they know and what bright suggestions they have.

LOW- AND MID-LEVEL PEOPLE HAVE GREAT INSIGHTS—IF YOU ASK THEM

It's a mindset opposed to the one of CFAs who see a company solely via its Value Line numbers (Buffett's favorite summary page, by the way) and the printed squiggles in the financial statements. Sure, the latter matter, and you should know them cold. But they definitely do not contain *all* the information—often the most important information of all. Luckily, 99% of CFA investors do not bother to ask employees. So if you do, you'll take the CFAs' money.

What did IBM's people tell me?

Oh, boy, did they have a lot to tell. Especially when I asked about the CEO and the chairman. In short, I got an earful. So let me just summarize.

CHAIRMAN ONCE GAVE AWAY THE STORE

IBM's then-chairman was (and is) notorious for allegedly signing the deal with Bill Gates to supply the software for IBM's personal computer, which was then in its infancy. Allegedly, the then-CEO neglected to put in the contract a second-supplier clause—that is, a right to have someone else supply the software, not just Microsoft, or at least, have partial rights to Microsoft's software. As a result, Bill Gates walked away with a practical monopoly on IBM's future PC business—IBM's *numero uno* growth segment.

How's that for commercial acumen?

Of course, Bill Gates could have refused such a request. He could have insisted that the rights to the software remain with Microsoft alone. But IBM's then-chairman was in such a good position to demand at least a share in the future bonanza that the fact that he (allegedly) didn't, handed away billions of IBM's market capitalization to MSFT. Just like that. And it was this very same chairman (whose name I omit here out of delicacy) who allegedly elevated the company's top saleswoman to president—even though sales were stagnant and declining.

Did I say acumen? The employees sure didn't.

SHARE BUYBACK IN A SHRINKING, SICK BUSINESS

At that same time, IBM was buying back its own shares, to shrink their number and so maintain growth in earnings per share (an important ink-squiggle for CFA types), convinced that its stock was undervalued. And yes, Warren Buffett does often recommend this practice. But it is suitable only in a healthy company, and IBM was certainly not that. Sales were stagnating, R&D ideas were not being acted on, or if they were, there was no R&D focus. And after all is said and done, *the basis of all strategy is focus*: you can't shoot in all directions. You must decide where to focus your R&D dollars, and IBM apparently didn't know, because it was run by salespeople, not visionary techies, like Apple and Microsoft. Or that, at least, is what I got from even low- and mid-level IBM people.

Small wonder then, that employees were unhappy, and management was not held in high regard, either by employees or by Wall Street. Although the latter didn't say so. Because if they did, they would have lost their "access" to top management, and then how would they know what earnings to forecast? ...

In short, it was one sick company—as most employees knew. But did Warren Buffett and Charlie Munger know this? Did this figure in their value calculations? Or was the Value Line summary-page of IBM's financials, book value, revenue per share, EPS, and other numbers, enough to show them "value?"

Apparently not. It seems Warren and Charlie did their value analysis *by the numbers*, as Ben Graham recommended.

Yes, BRK also has the concept of a "moat," that prevents competitors from storming the company's business. It is a concept introduced by Buffett (though it might've been by Munger), but IBM didn't have a strong moat, *as its employees knew*. Buffett apparently only *thought* IBM did; but it didn't.

SECURITY ANALYSIS IS NOT COMPANY ANALYSIS

This miss, in fact, is typical for most Graham and Dodd fans: Ben Graham's Security Analysis speaks only about the *security*, the stock, which is the fictional reflection of the physical company. It never speaks about the company itself or of its people.

But it's not just people information that's behind the sleuthing method. Rather, it's the mindset that *not all information can be encapsulated in ink squiggles and screen blips*—whether about people, the world, or the universe at large.

However, in IBM's case, the key to its sleuthing was the reviews I got from IBM people about their CEO. Because these were often worse than those I got for the chairman.

BELOW-AVERAGE PEOPLE SKILLS, BELOW-AVERAGE MANAGEMENT ABILITY

Yes, she was a good salesperson, but some of the contracts she got were allegedly with ho-hum margins, and her people skills were average or below. And there was more, which I will leave out. But the upshot was, I went back to friends and old partners who had asked for my opinion, and told them that no matter how much IBM stock Warren and Charlie had bought based on published numbers, IBM was a sick company and should be avoided.

Within a year, two events happened that justified the sleuthed information.

CEO SAYS 10% OF IBM PEOPLE UNDER PAR

First, the CEO announced that 10% of the company's employees had not kept up their tech skills, and now would have two years to upgrade them. Those who could not, would not stay.

This was too foolish for words. Because, not surprisingly, morale among IBMers plunged immediately, as it became known as "the tech company with under-par people." It was as if all IBMers now had an invisible scarlet 10% figure on their foreheads, for everyone outside IBM—and also those inside—to see, as all wondered who were those under-par…

Not surprisingly, the job of IBM recruiters became instantly harder. Because who wants to work for a company with under-par tech people?

And, of course, the really *above*-par people immediately began to send out their resumes.

Was any of this in the Value Line numbers? Was any of this in Wall Street reports? Or in Warren's and Charlie's due diligence? Did any of them bother to talk to the low-level engineers —the equivalents of Rene McPherson's machinist—that I had talked to? None I had talked to ever said they did.

Then a second, and worse thing happened.

CEO WANTS TO BRING THE APPLE FOX INTO IBM'S HENHOUSE

IBM's then-CEO met Apple's Steve Jobs, went for a well-photographed stroll with him, and floated the idea of having Apple's R&D people meet those at IBM.

At this idea, the unprintable words escalated. Because Steve Jobs was known as the enterprising guy who legally stole Xerox's mouse and WYSIWYG (What You See is What You Get) screen technology from PARC (Palo Alto Research Centre), where he was taken for a walk by Xerox's obtuse management.

Xerox at the time—like IBM when I sleuthed it—had tons of good technology which its management was too inept to commercialize and was not yet patented, so Steve Jobs pounced on it, got back to his office, and called a designer to make for him the first computer mouse. A few months later he made the first WYSIWYG screen.

Apple blossomed, and Xerox shrank.

TALKING TO THE COMPETITOR'S THIEF IN CHIEF

So now here was IBM's CEO proposing to bring in this famous thieving fox into IBM's henhouse, to talk to IBM's pregnant R&D hens—so he could steal their R&D golden eggs! This showed not only stupidity, but also disrespect for IBM's R&D people, who were publicly shown as needing a boost of creativity by talking to their winning competitor's thief in chief!

If there had been any doubt that the unprintable words IBM's people said about their management had been apt, it was now dispelled.

What surprised me, and my friends and former partners, was the slowness of all this to penetrate the ken of value investors who bought IBM stock: both Berkshire, and piggy-backing investors who tagged along on Warren and Charlie's coattails.

BRK FINALLY SELLS IBM AT A SMALL LOSS

In 2018, full seven years after Berkshire had bought IBM stock, it finally sold it, at $140/share, or an 18% loss.

Now, as investment losses go, -18% in seven years isn't terrible—it's about -2.5% per year, or roughly equal to the dividend yield, i.e., the loss was almost a wash. Which goes to show that for investment geniuses (for Buffett surely is one), even losses are remarkable in their mildness. Goodness knows I've had worse, and so did Berkshire occasionally. For example, its foray into airlines, which Charlie Munger mentioned as a mistake, pointing out that airlines are a bad business in general, as an industry.

Still, a loss is a loss, and one should learn from it. What can we learn from Berkshire's IBM foray?

IBM'S BUSINESS WAS NOT BAD; THE COMPANY ITSELF WAS

IBM's industry, tech and computers, is certainly *not* a bad business, like airlines are. Some tech businesses, like Microsoft's, have the deepest moats around them. In fact, Charlie Munger is known to own some MSFT shares personally. Rather, IBM, the company *itself* and the way it was run (or not run), was bad. Most employees could tell you this, if you only asked them. But Warren and Charlie apparently didn't.

Why not?

This of course I don't know. Both are far, far smarter (and richer) than I am, so the most likely answer is that their worldview (as that of almost every value investor and CFA), is that a company's financial statements and footnotes, if carefully read, contain *all* the information you need to make an investment decision.

PHYSICISTS GUILTY OF SAME BLIND VIEW

That view, incidentally, is also the view of physicists: that all information about the universe can be contained in ink squiggles that denote categories. It is an ancient view, also known as *reductionism.* If you are a CFA-type investor, e.g., Jim O'Shaughnessy, who picks stocks strictly by their valuation numbers, or Joel Greenblatt, who picks stocks via their EVA numbers, or Ben Graham in his day, then you too are a Reductionist, even though you are not aware of it.

This idea is so important for your sleuthing success that I'd better explain it using an old parable.

2,400 years old, to be exact.

CHAPTER 5

MATHEMATICIANS' POINT OF VIEW

Ignoramus vs. Ignorabimus: your black-and-white brain in Plato's cave.

Socrates relates a parable (which he attributes to Plato) of wise men having been chained to a cave wall all their lives, with their faces to the wall, so that they have no way of watching the world outside. Luckily, though, there's a fire (or a sun) outside, which throws shadows of the outside world on the cave's wall, and these the chained men can see—and give names to.

These shadows and their names are, for the men, *representations* of the world outside—it's all they can see.

CAN THE WORLD BE FULLY KNOWN BY ITS SHADOWS?

The question is:

How much of the *real* world can the chained men *know* via its shadowy representations?

In philosophy, this question is known as **reductionism**. It is usually phrased as: How much of the world can we know via its *categories*, which are the *names* we give to our sensory representations of the world: small /

big, loud / quiet, black / white, red / blue, soft / hard, sour / sweet, fast / slow, right / left...?

And an even better question is: Which parts of the real world (if any) would *evade* us, once we have *replaced our sensory perceptions with names, i.e., words and numbers*?

That of course is a key question in physics, although physicists do not like it mentioned, since no discipline likes to dwell on its limitations; it's also a key question in the case of math, and (as you must by now realize) is also key in the case of accounting—which is the base of all that CFAs do, and in essence is the underlying topic of this book.

PHYSICISTS CHANGED THE DEFINITION

Even though this chapter is a lesson from mathematicians' point of view, we must say here something about physicists' point of view, too. Because, since they disliked the topic so much, they slyly modified the definition of reductionism into "big things are made of small things," which of course is not the same thing at all, since in the inner-brain domain of reductionism, there are no "things"—that's for the outside world, which we (the cave dwellers) cannot experience directly. We only perceive the outside world's *attributes*, as they're represented by squiggly ink on paper or chalk marks on board (also known by Einstein as Formalism) of either words or numbers or pictures or charts.

So back to Plato's cave, and the original definition of reductionism, since it is relevant to our purpose of taking CFAs' money: **How much of the real world of commerce can we know from its inky representations on financial statements and price charts, and how much is left out? And if so, which parts?**

This question—about the world as a whole, not just commerce—appears in math in various guises. Let's get into a few here, just to make clear what you, as a sleuth investor, are faced with. And to do this, let's start simple.

KOLMOGOROV'S COMPLEXITY AND DARK INFO

A famed Russian mathematician by the name of Andrey Kolmogorov, asked the following: *How to measure the complexity of a string of numbers?*

For our purpose, we'll restate his question as follows: *How much information does a string of numbers contain, and how to measure it?*

This question is naturally related to *our quest for the holy investment grail, the Dark Information*, the kind that *cannot* be contained in a string of numbers (or letters), and so *cannot be named.*

For example: How much *commercial* info can a company's financial statements contain? And the obvious corollary, what's *not* containable in these numbers? Getting at such un-nameable information would be our secret weapon of taking OPM (Other People's Money), and, as you'll see, this info is luckily kept in a part of your brain which you can access via sleuthing.

And so, in order to get at this goldmine, we restate Kolmogorov's answer as follows:

KOLMOGOROV'S COMPLEXITY, RESTATED

A string can be said to contain information, if (using a specific programming language, or even just language) we can condense it to a *shorter* string *which lets us reconstruct* the first string.

Both these parts ('shorter' and 'reconstruct') are necessary.

For simplicity's sake, assume that the original string is composed of 1s and 0s only. And, let's say it's a string of 100 bits. Say the string is 50 1s followed by 50 0s. Then, the sentence "50 1s followed by 50 0s" has just reduced the original string to a string of 23 bits (including spaces).

We can now reconstruct the original 100-bit string, via the above 23-bit string. The original 100-bit string can then be said to have information, because it has *patterns*, or *categories.*

DESCRIPTIVE VS. PRESCRIPTIVE

However, please note that the second, shorter string, is not just *descriptive* of the first string, but also *prescriptive.* That is, it lets us *reconstruct* the first string *exactly.*

An important side-question is in order here:

Are the financial statements of a company equal to the above type of "condensed second string?" That is, can we *reconstruct* the entire company's commercial essence *strictly* based on its financial statements?

This question, as you'll see later, is a kissing cousin of the Turing Test, which asks whether a string of ink squiggles can contain the entire essence of an entity's "humanness." But let's not jump too far ahead. One string at a time. Back to Kolmogorov.

Obviously, the answer to the above question is No. There are many other attributes to a company, some categorizable, others not, that do *not* appear in its financial statements.

MAKING THE FIRST STEP TOWARDS THE "DARK INFO"

The obvious follow-up question then is:

What critical company info are we missing? Please put down a potential list of what this missing info can be. It'd be a good start for what to sleuth for later. But let's stay for the moment with Kolmogorov.

Let's assume now that we *cannot* find any pattern in the first, original string, that allows us to describe it *prescriptively* by a shorter one.

Can we then definitely say that there *aren't any* such shorter, prescriptive strings for it?

That's a very good question without easy answers. Because, first, how many hours have we tried? And, second, how many hours do we *need* to try, to be able to say there's *no way* to compress the first string? That is, that there are *no* patterns, or *categories*, in the first string?

Quite clearly, as the original first string gets longer, the above question becomes practically unanswerable. All we can say, then, is that it *appears highly likely* that the first string is *uncategorized.*

But is it also *uncategorizable*?

That we do not know. We can only say that, with a high level of certainty, that first string has no categories, and therefore it is *random.*

KOLMOGOROV RANDOMNESS

But please note that this randomness is of a particular kind: *Kolmogorov randomness*. Because, note also that this "second string" is now *descriptive*, not *prescriptive*. In other words, unlike the first compression of the 100-bit string, which enabled us to *reconstruct* the first string *exactly* in its entirety, this second description (saying "the string is Kolmogorov-random"), does *not* enable us to reconstruct the first string, because saying "a string is

Kolmogorov-random," only says it *appears* to have no categories (i.e., that we could find none in our limited time), and so it is (apparently) *a category of its own*, i.e., a sui-generis, a one-of-a-kind (as far as we can see).

But (you're probably saying now), why is all this important? How is this tied to our attempt to find the Dark Information that cannot be named and so cannot be contained in a company's financial statements, and so can be used to take CFA-investors' money?

Let's get back then to Plato's cave.

We are facing the wall and are looking at it. There are shadows dancing on the wall.

THE INTERNET AS A BLACK AND WHITE KOLMOGOROV CATEGORIZER

Unbeknownst to us, though, the world outside is in full color. (It has other attributes too, of smell and taste and touch, but let's keep it simple.) Also, and unknown to us, the wall before us has special qualities: it is a computer screen that can only show black and white.

However, the outside world streams into the cave a continuous string of sunlight of *all* wavelengths, full color, full spectrum. (Forget about the smell and such.) Therefore, the input to the wall-screen are numbers of *all* values and sizes. Integers and irrational numbers and everything else in between.

So, in order to translate this outside world's numbers-stream to the limited abilities of the screen, there is a *pre*-screen "translator" chip that takes in all the outside numerical data, and converts it to 1s and 0s only. That is, into distinct *categories.*

How does this translation work?

Anything above a certain threshold, T, will be 1, and so appear as a white pixel. Anything below T will be 0, and therefore appear as a black pixel.

As a result, while we are imprisoned in the cave (which the Greeks made clear is a parable of our body, whose senses let us perceive the non-body world), the full splendor of the real world behind us is invisible to us. All we can see is the black and white *translation* of the 1s and 0s.

In other words, we see a long string of 1s and 0s as the *(categorized) information* about the "real world's" (uncategorized) data, and these 1s and 0s, for us, *are* the world, even though the world's "true numbers" are much more varied—perhaps even infinitely so.

CORTEX WORKS AS TRANSLATOR INTO CATEGORIES

Now let's talk about the Kolmogorov translator chip (which, as you'll see later in the chapter about brain science, is a parable for our cortex):

Can our brain find patterns in this chip's output—the black and white 1s and 0s string—which are the "shadows" on our brain's screen wall?

It sure can.

Some patterns our brain calls trees, others it calls stars, others still grass, or flowers. Some it may even call inventory, or apartment buildings. And others still appear to have no patterns at all (and so, naturally, no names).

Of course, the fact that black-and-white pictures are only a thin distillation of the original full-color (and full-other-things) world is unknown to us, except as a theoretical possibility. (We may be imprisoned in the cave, but we are no dummies and can still think intelligently.)

The question now is:

Can we somehow access the *pre-compression* information of the original string, so as to get the full colors of the world outside? Even though our brain can only see black and white?

Why do we need it?

"SYSTEM 2" INVESTING AS BLACK AND WHITE TRANSLATION

Assume that, to pass the time, all of us chained-to-the-wall sages are betting on which shadow will move (or rise) fastest. The only info we have is the named B&W shadows. Obviously, if some of us had access to the *pre-sifted* info, we could win all the others' money and become rich.

But, can we get this info? And if so, how?

That, of course, is a clear hint at the question of how to get the *physical information* of a company, which can *not* be contained in the financial statements—which, in turn, are a sort of Kolmogorov compression of the full-color physical splendor of the pageant of commerce into categorized B&W debits and credits.

This compression of commerce into financial statements was first performed around five hundred years ago by Luca Pacioli, in his invention of accounting—which is nothing less than seeing the drama of human commerce via the thin Turing slot of numbers and categories.

"SYSTEM 1" THINKING IS ABOUT THE FULL COLORS LEFT OUT

But what has been left out, after shoehorning commerce into financial statements? Which parts of commerce are *not* in Pacioli's three dials?

We already saw that people are missing. But what else is?

That, of course, is the jackpot question. Because while CFA types use "System 2" thinking to invest via the debits and credits system, somewhere in our brain may also exist the raw, uncategorized data about commerce, with which we might do amazing things (maybe) via "System 1" thinking.

If only we could access it!

But how, exactly? And where is it stored?

Let's stay with the math metaphor and go forward in time, much after Plato, but still in the past.

WHAT WE CAN KNOW, AND WHAT WE CAN'T. OR CAN WE?

In 1900 a big mathematics conference took place in Paris. It was attended by the world's most famous mathematicians of the day, who came to feast on French cuisine, visit Paris' disorderly houses (to use Proust's term), exchange gossip about the latest math theories, and present papers. The conference was led by David Hilbert, the foremost mathematician of the day and perhaps one of the top mathematicians of the entire 20th century, who also gave the keynote speech.

In his speech, Hilbert presented 23 problems, none of which was proven or disproven at the time. Solving them, he said, would advance math, science and human knowledge (all of which seemed to merge in his mind into one). In the 122 years since, several of the problems have been laid to rest, either proven correct or disproven. But a few problems, oddly, were found to be unprovable—that is, they were neither true nor untrue—*within math*. And that's because, as was found 30 years *after* the conference, math had a big hole in it, so some things it could not do. And one of the things it couldn't do was probe its own limitations.

But I am jumping too far ahead.

First off, why do I mention all this in a book meant to help you outperform the market by taking CFAs' money?

For two reasons.

SIMILAR LIMITATIONS TO MATH AND ACCOUNTING

First, because the 1900 math congress brings to mind *the obvious parallel between math and accounting*. Math is accepted as the exclusive language of science (or at least it was so, until recently, when quantum physics found extra holes in it), while accounting is the language of business (Warren Buffett said so explicitly). It, too (as sleuthing theory is finding), has big holes in it (for example: the absence of people). What's more, just like math, accounting is also unable to probe its own limitations *while using only its own method.*

So that's one: comparing math's incompleteness to accounting's incompleteness.

PROBING THE LIMITATIONS BY GOING OUTSIDE MATH—AND ACCOUNTING

But second and more practical: if you are a mathematician-investor, this story of the 1900 math conference should help you realize that numerical data in the financial statements do not—cannot—contain *all* business information, just as it has been proven that math cannot contain all science information. (Although that last part of "has been proven," we'll see only in the chapter from physicists' point of view.) And once you are convinced of *that*, you'd then be much more likely to turn off your internet screen and go out to sleuth for original, *physical* info, if you want to outperform the market. Which is the aim of this book.

But how can you tell what's missing (in either math or accounting), if it cannot be done within the discipline's system?

Yes, you'd have to go out of the system. But go out how?

We'll get to that very soon. However, first one more side-bar:

HILBERT'S 23 CENTENNIAL PROBLEMS

If you are not a mathematician, and are curious to know what these 23 questions were, look them up on Wikipedia, or Google, or any other search engine. Just key in "Hilbert 23 problems." Luckily, of the 23, only three (DH#1, DH#2, and DH#6) are relevant to the main claim of this book, which is that *math, and indeed all symbol systems (including language, among which is accounting), unknowingly miss much of what's going on. And* they miss stuff because they're slaves to the younger part of the human brain, the cortex, *which categorizes— and names—all sensory input so as to apply logic and reason and math to the resulting names, and so be able to forecast (slowly) what's coming.*

However: By doing so, the cortex must first *discard* what it could *not* categorize, so there's always a part of the world of which it is unaware.

CATEGORIES ARE INVENTED BY THE CORTEX

Now, you may ask: Why the need for categories? For example, in accounting?

Because, just like in Plato's cave, the brain applies "System 2" math and logic *not* to the world itself, but to its own *self-invented names* of the world—the shadows on your brain's wall.

Therefore, if the real universe (including the commercial one) has regions which *cannot* be represented by categories, (which are only the invention of the brain's cortex anyway), then there's no math in these regions either, and you'd have to use something *else* there to make forecasts. For example, about stocks.

And what is this something else? Because maybe it can still be part of math? Say if we *modify* math somehow?

YOU CAN'T HANDLE NON-MATH WITH MATH SYMBOLS

Since this is a chapter from mathematicians' point of view (and those interested in math), I permit myself to mention that a certain ex-Harvard and ex-Princeton genius named Jacob Lurie has been trying for the last few years to invent a new kind of math *without* categories, by exchanging the "equal" sign for an "equivalent" sign.

However, by so doing, Lurie in effect admits that there's something else which math cannot capture, and therefore *math has to limit itself to equivalence only*. No equality.

Can you imagine what would happen if physics did this too? For example, if Schrödinger's equation changed its equality into equivalence, thus admitting that some parts of its input *cannot be expressed in ink-squiggles (aka variables)*? And so, effectively, admitting that its famous cat cannot be both alive and dead?

This, in effect, is already happening (arguably), but it is for the next chapter from physicists' point of view to discuss.

SHADES OF GÖDEL

For the moment, however, we only claim that the same also holds for equations of accounting, and value investing, and CFA stuff. That is, *neither can accounting contain all info, nor can it be modified from within to contain what it cannot.*

Or maybe Lurie's effort can still enable us—one day—to make accounting handle this non-accounting stuff too? Like his attempt to make math contain non-categories also? (Hint: he divides each category into infinitely small parts, maybe taking a page out of calculus.)

The answer is no.

Lurie's effort is almost certainly futile, because by trying to investigate non-categories using math ink squiggles, which *themselves* are categories, he very likely makes himself into a sort of modern-day Bertrand Russell and Alfred North Whitehead. They were a pair of early 20th century mathematicians whose book *Principia Mathematica*, all three volumes of it, tried to answer Hilbert Question #2, but was shown to be bunk by a genius named Kurt Gödel (who was also Einstein's best friend, and, according to Einstein, just as smart).

Gödel by the way was also present in that 1900 Paris conference (though he didn't say much), and 30 years after it, he overturned David Hilbert's blind faith in math, with a nine-page paper pointing out the famous math hole, which also sank Russell and Whitehead's book.

You can read more about Gödel's paper in Nagel and Newman's marvelous little book about Gödel's theorem. (See glossary of books.)

But, jumping the gun again (for the physicists), in a very similar way to Gödel's finding, Jacob Lurie's work (called Higher Category Theory), had likely already been nullified by the work of John Stewart Bell, a sort of modern day Gödel (in physics) who showed that in the seam between classical physics and quantum physics, variables (that is, categories) do not exist. And this was proven experimentally several times over, at a high-confidence level (6-sigma and 13-sigma if you want to know). So if Gödel (now in math heaven) is following what's happening down here on earth, he's probably looking at Lurie's work and chuckling. And so is Hilbert, probably, as are Russell and Whitehead, though ruefully.

However, once again I'm jumping too far ahead.

Back to the 1900 Paris conference, and to its most memorable event, after Hilbert's speech.

Right after that speech, once Hilbert had presented his 23 problems whose solution would advance human knowledge, someone asked him diffidently whether there was perhaps a limit to human knowledge.

Because maybe there are things we *cannot* know? Know via math, that is.

TWO KINDS OF IGNORANCE

This question, all immediately understood, sprang from a book by one Emil du Bois-Reymond, a German physiologist (that is, an expert on the human body) published in 1870, thirty years *before* that Paris conference. In that book, and in a later talk ("On the limits of natural sciences") Bois-Reymond presented the idea of two kinds of ignorance: *Ignoramus* and *ignorabimus*. Which translate from Latin as we *do not* know, and we *cannot* know.

In other words, Dark Information exists.

Although Bois-Reymond did not frame his expression this way, his field of study allows us to assume that he referred to our brain—i.e., some things our brain simply *cannot* know.

That of course was a huge claim—setting a *biological* limit to science and scientific knowledge. So David Hilbert was incensed. No, he cried out, I strongly believe we can know everything! *We must know, and we will know*! He said it in German, by the way, and his words became famous (they are on his tombstone): *Wir müssen wissen — wir werden wissen!*

Thirty years after that, in 1930, right after Gödel had stated his explosive thesis about math's incompleteness, Hilbert, in a famous radio address, repeated the sentence—which was, in essence, the sum of his life's work: *Humans can know everything via science, whose tool is mathematics.*

HILBERT'S FAITH WAS REDUCTIONISM

But Hilbert was wrong, of course, although he didn't know it yet, because math, science's tool (as Gödel found), is flawed.

To Hilbert's credit, he didn't state his credo as a provable rule, but only as a private belief. This belief was that the orderly manipulation of ink squiggles on paper (or chalk marks on board), has the ability to tell us humans (or rather the cortex in our brains) *everything* about nature.

In other words, science (for Hilbert at least) was implicitly reductionism writ large.

Or, stated explicitly: Ink squiggles on paper can contain ***all*** *properties of the Universe*, and ***although we are not <u>yet</u> smart enough to know them all, one day*** *(so goes the belief),* ***we will.***

I'm jumping the gun here again, to note that the same reasoning, of "not knowing *yet*, but one day we could," (i.e., *ignoramus* yes, *ignorabimus* no), was used several years later by Einstein and two colleagues (Podolsky and Rosen). The trio hypothesised "hidden variables" (in Schrödinger's equation, yes) to explain a mystery where two different categories (e.g., two particles) fly apart from each other but still behave like one category ("entangled"), and so give the semblance of "spooky action at a distance," i.e., at faster-than-light speed.

HILBERT'S BELIEF SIMILAR TO EINSTEIN'S—AND BOTH WERE WRONG. OR WERE THEY?

This, or what became known as the EPR paradox (see later in the physicists' viewpoint chapter), was also related to reductionism. Because the alternative—that there are *no* hidden variables, arguably meant that *in some areas of physics* (in the seam between quantum and classical), *there are perhaps no variables* at all, i.e., there are domains of physics, i.e., the Universe, probably immune to be handled by math.

Provable at 13-sigma level, let's remind the physicists among you. Which is as close to a certainty (in physics) as you can get.

And which of course—in this book—is a parable for all commercial info that *accounting* cannot handle, because some areas of commerce (*contra* Pacioli, and *contra* Graham and Dodd), just like the seam between classical physics and quantum physics, are immune to "commercial math" also.

And now, another short sidebar.

Because before we proceed to practical conclusions for your sleuthing, we should focus briefly on the three of Hilbert's Problems relevant to our theme of *non-reductionism as key to the Dark Info*.

HILBERT'S PROBLEMS #1, #2, AND #6

The three relevant Hilbert Problems are:

Hilbert problem #1, or DH#1, the so-called **Continuum hypothesis**, comparing small and large infinities (I kid you not), via something called Cardinality (which is a mushy word for "size" when infinities are concerned.)

DH#2, aiming to **develop mathematics from first axioms**, as the Greeks did to geometry; and as Russell and Whitehead tried to do, before Gödel did them in (alas). And,

DH#6, aiming to **axiomatize physics**. That, is, prove that physics, or the Universe at large, can be entirely comprehended via categories, like geometry can (which the Greeks did), or math (which can't, as Gödel later showed), i.e., reductionism lives in the Universe, as per Hilbert.

So, again, one more time: Why is all this important to sleuthing?

Because if there are regions in the world (including the commercial world) where there are *no* categories, no matter what your (categorizing) cortex says, then there's no math (or accounting) there either. So in that strange place, there's no physics (or accounting) of the type that your (and CFAs') cortex understands, with math and measurements and such, since math requires categories. Which unfortunately there just aren't. So CFA stuff won't work there either.

Therefore, if sleuthing *would* work there, then…

WHAT ARE CATEGORIES?

But wait. We need one more segue before we go on: Because, if you are neither a mathematician nor a physicist, we should first define for you that over-used word.

What *is* a category?

In physics, as in accounting, a category is an entity or quality that is **distinct** from others, that **varies**, and can be **measured**. (In liberal arts that last bit doesn't hold. But we are not in the liberal arts. Yet.) Once the category is defined, it can be *named* and *replaced by a variable*—which is an ink squiggle (or computer bit, or screen blip), like X or Y or M, or Assets, and so on. That's now the category's *name*.

The *name*, please note. Not the category itself, only its name. And *both are purely the invention of your cortex*. Nothing to do with the real, non-categories world. An invention, nothing more.

And oh, yes. Please note one more thing:

When you write X, or Working Capital, or Mass as a category's name, you only denote the category in *general* by naming it. You then only know that it's *distinct* from *other* categories. Such as categories Y, P, and Debt. But you still do not know its *size*.

CATEGORY NAME FIRST, MEASUREMENT SECOND

However, you also know it *can* be measured (because it is not in the liberal arts). But you don't know its measure (value) *yet*.

That measurement requires a *willful act*, and it's relevant especially for physics and also for sleuthing, in both of which it matters *a lot*, and is really the crux of almost everything sleuths do. Especially when we want to take OPM (i.e., Other People's Money) in the market.

What is *measurement*, then?

It is the quadruple act of (1) willfully choosing a category to (2) denote a physical event or entity then (3) naming it, and (4) exchanging the name with a squiggle denoting a specific number. This last number-squiggle, in turn, represents a *multiple* of this measured quantity compared to a *standard quantity*.

For example, the measurement (value) of the (chosen category) length L of a ruler, can be represented by the squiggle 3, which means that this particular length is three times bigger than the length of the standard meter made of platinum, sitting in Sèvres (a Parisian suburb) in France. Or a cash pile of $1,000, that is 1,000 x the value of a one-dollar bill, which is the agreed unit of commercial value, same as the meter is the agreed unit of length.

Physics (which will appear in the next chapter) is similarly composed of many such (willful) measurements of real events' (chosen) categories, exchanging the events' names by squiggles denoting measurable variables.

The pre-measurement variables (that is, their names) are connected by math symbols like plus, minus, multiplied, divide, raised to a power, integrals, sigma, equal, etc. These name-squiggles are manipulated so as to arrive (via a predetermined process) at another squiggle that, hopefully, will forecast the size of a future real event, represented by the squiggle that the formulae had come up with, and so forecasted.

SCIENCE AND CFA INVESTING ARE FORECASTING VIA SQUIGGLES

And that, in effect, is science: *the manipulation of squiggles denoting categories, so as to forecast a real event.* Which, of course, is also a good definition of CFA-type investing. It's all done via squiggles, as O'Shaughnessy, Greenblatt, and Ben Graham demonstrate. Because accounting, just like physics, is done via named categories, exchanged for number squiggles.

But can squiggles capture the *entirety* of the universe? Or, for our purpose, of the *commercial* universe? That is, the world of stocks, and the market?

There's more about it in the chapter meant to convince physicists to get out and sleuth.

For the moment, though, what you should take away from all this is that reductionism (the Greek kind), or at least the implicit *belief* in it, is not only the basis of classic math, and classical physics, but is also the basis of all classical "*security* analysis" (again, *security*, not company). And this is **the belief that the ink squiggles in financial statements represent all the qualities of the company in whose security you have an interest, and so the squiggles contain all the necessary *knowledge* about the company, to enable you to invest profitably**.

Necessary for your cortex, that is.

CFA'S ARE ALL REDUCTIONISTS REDUX

If you are studying for the CFA exam, this is a faith you must uphold. Because what value-investing CFAs do in their stock analysis, is pure stock market reductionism.

Which, as far as general mathematics went, was also how matters stood in Paris, circa 1900, and still did in 1930, when Hilbert gave his radio address, where he stated his credo, which, like Russell and Whitehead's book, had already been done-in by Gödel's paper.

Gödel's paper on the hole-inside-all-math had an immediate effect. Russell and Whitehead's book was already finished when Gödel's paper appeared as a thunderclap. That paper proved irrefutably that their book, all three volumes of it, was bunkum.

Why was it bunkum?

THE ANSWER TO DH#1 WAS A NO

Because *there are attributes of the real world that ink squiggles can not contain.* That statement is reflected in many word-based absurdities, such as, "this sentence is wrong," or, "the above italicized statement contains *all* true information about the real world." Or a piece of paper with a statement on both sides, both saying the statement on the *other* side is wrong.

The resulting sorry fact that math, science's universal tool, is (as mathematicians politely said) "incomplete" had repercussions, both in math and later in physics—and, I hope you'll see, henceforward in accounting and investing also.

So first off, Hilbert's first question was about the difference between sizes of infinity (cardinality). The question was: Can you prove that there is no other infinity between the smaller one (the number of integers) and the larger one (the number of points on a line segment)?

That was shown to be unprovable. That is, you can neither prove it is correct, nor that it is incorrect.

It is, in effect, outside of math.

THE ANSWER TO DH#2 IS A DEFINITE NO ALSO

Whether the symbol for infinity *itself* has any meaning outside the world of ink-squiggles, was left to be discussed by philosophers. However, this book is neither about philosophy, nor physics, nor math, but about money, and how you can get more of it by taking the other side of (some) CFAs' trades. Yet just to hammer the point home, Hilbert's second problem, regarding the development of math axiomatically, was answered with a definite No: Gödel showed this conclusively.

And so yes, du Bois-Reymond was right, and David Hilbert was wrong. Some things we cannot know via math. But not just *things* in the liberal arts, like beauty and justice and poetry, but also things in physics itself, that is science.

And it is also thus in commerce, and economics, and of course in stock analysis and research, which Pacioli's accounting claimed to have made into a science, but didn't.

In plain words, accounting (=commerce's math) is just as incomplete as math itself.

So what will complete it? And how?

Not to tease you any longer, the answer is: not the modern, categorizing part of your brain, that is, the cortex, that does "System 2" thinking, but rather the old, *un*evolved part of your brain, the portion that does Kahneman's faster, but not entirely accurate "System 1" thinking.

Which, yes, you *can* access, once you know how. Wait, and you'll see.

PHYSICS: KNOWING (OR BEING ABLE TO FORECAST) THE UNIVERSE'S EVENTS

To get there, we must delve into DH#6 a bit, which we'll do in Chapter 8.

But just to make sure you see what the issue is:

In his sixth problem, Hilbert asked whether it was possible to develop physics axiomatically, the same way that Hilbert #2 asked this about math.

Or, to be precise: Hilbert asked *two* things in this problem. First, whether it was possible to develop physics' probability theory for the macro world, and second, whether it was possible to do so for the quanta world (as Hilbert called it)—that is, physics of the minutest size.

Both will serve as useful analogies—with very practical implications—to what can be done (or not done) with accounting, so as to take CFAs' money.

We'll leave that problem for chapter 8 (from physicists' point of view) and meantime sum up what we saw in this chapter of mathematicians' viewpoint which is applicable to your sleuthing arts.

CONCLUSIONS REGARDING SLEUTHING:

Your main tool for investing is your brain. This is also the tool of your opponents.

However, **a brain is not a neutral tool**. It is composed of a cortex, which is the newest part, and much older parts: the limbic system, the brain stem, and more.

Your cortex takes in sensory data and converts it to categories, which can be named and used, to do math and accounting on. However, both accounting and math are blind to non-categories—which is where sleuths' information edge lies.

When the cortex extracts categories from incoming sensory data, **it discards what could not be categorized**. So this part of the incoming data is unseen by the cortex—*and therefore also by CFAs*. That's what we sleuths seek.

It's not easy to access this hidden brain where the Dark Info resides, but it is possible. And if you know how to, and do, you can take CFAs' money, whose cortex is blind to any info outside the financial statements' ink and bits.

CHAPTER 6
LAWYERS' POINT OF VIEW

Judge Turing's test for a key witness, and the Internet as a Turing slot.

And now for a short interlude.

Assume you are an introvert, hate to talk to people, and would rather pay someone to append a company's "people info" to its financials, for which you'll be happy to pay.

Could it be done?

NO AUDITOR FOR PEOPLE INFO

Even if it could be, what kind of info would you want included, and whose? Just the C-Suite's exec's names and their CVs? What of their professional weaknesses? Or personal flaws? Come to think of it, where would you get such info? And *how could you be sure it is correct*?

In the matter of financial statements, you at least have an auditor who testifies to the numbers' truth and accuracy. But what about people info? Who would be the auditor there? Or can there be one? Especially if the info is gleaned from the Internet? How can you be sure it's not lies, or Wall Street PR masquerading as "research," aiming to take *your* money, on behalf of their CFA clients?

All are important questions. So just to make sure you don't skip this chapter and go right to the end (or the physics chapter), here's a short fable which I hope will stick in your memory every time you're tempted to click on the Buy or Sell button based only on Internet "information."

JUDGE TURING'S COURT PROCEDURE

Assume you are a top defense lawyer, one Percival Mason, Esq., hired to defend millionaire investor Charles A. Boffin against charges that he runs a crooked set of books and is a front for the mob.

Your client denies this indignantly. He's innocent, he says. Rather it is the District Attorney (who is prosecuting the case himself) who's the crook here. The DA wants a perfect record of never having lost a case, and so has faked the evidence against Mr. Boffin. Yes, says your client, the DA cheats.

The DA rejects this claim with disdain. The government, he insists, will prove the charges against Mr. Boffin beyond any smidgen of doubt.

But what is the government's actual evidence? you ask.

Since the DA must tell you this, he reveals that a team of government forensic accountants have pored over Mr. Boffin's books and found some debits and credits that did not seem to add up.

This, you say with equal disdain, is not enough. To convict, you need real evidence, not just circumstantial. Real, as in physical. And do you?

Yes, says the DA. The government has recruited a whistleblower in Mr. Boffin's organization, who has agreed to testify on condition of absolute anonymity. No photos of his or her face, no drawings, not even a hint about his or her background. And not even his/her voice, even if electronically changed, which he/she fears that the mob could identify.

So how will he (or she) testify? you ask.

In writing, says the DA.

Oh no, you say. We have to cross-examine him or her.

No way, says the DA. It entails too much risk to the witness.

You argue back and forth, and finally you bring the problem to the judge, the Honorable A. Turing, who decides that, to hide the whistleblower's identity, the witness shall answer your written questions via a slot in the courtroom's wall.

Which language would the witness prefer? he asks.

The DA says it doesn't matter. The witness speaks dozens of languages perfectly, so the defense can choose. The witness prefers not to specify any, for fear of being identified.

You still object, but the judge insists. Both Mr. Boffin's rights and the whistleblower's safety must be preserved. Querying the whistleblower through the wall's slot is the way it'll happen.

The day of trial arrives.

However, on the morning of the trial, your detective, Ms. Sleutzky, grabs you by the arm on the courthouse's steps, and whispers in your ear that one of her informers inside the DA's office just told her that the DA's witness is not human. He/she/it is really an AI program that had pored over Mr. Boffin's books, and will be answering questions as if it is human, to lend the responses extra credibility.

In other words: your client was right. The DA indeed cheats. But since your detective cannot divulge how she's learned this—her informer fears for his job, perhaps his life— it's an impasse. However, as an experienced lawyer, you do see here an angle for the defense.

With utmost courtesy, you ask the Hon. Judge: Can the DA formally assure the defense that the witness is human, and not an electronic construct that pretends to be human? Because, as per Supreme Court decision in the case of Asimov vs. R. Daneel, an AI cannot testify against humans.

The DA huffs and puffs. What kind of an objection is that? he says. *We* don't have to prove anything. *You* go ahead and prove to the court that the informer is *not* human.

No way, you say. This is America. My client doesn't have to prove his innocence. Rather, you have to prove his guilt via *human* testimony, not via an AI, no matter how clever it is.

You and the DA go back and forth, while the Honorable Judge eats an apple and ponders.

At last, the judge decides. Since the interests of your client and of the witness clash, both are at risk. He'll let the defense (you) query the witness first, via the slot in the courtroom's wall about *any* topic, even unrelated to the case, so as to try to prove to the court that the whistleblower (he/she/it) is indeed *not* human.

Then the DA would be allowed to have a go, to prove that the witness *is* human.

As the court clerk steps up to the wall's slot, followed by a trio of translators, the issues before the court are three:

What questions can the defense ask to prove that the witness is *not* human?

What questions can the prosecutor ask, to prove that he or she *is*?

Can *either* task be done beyond reasonable doubt, within a limited time?

Let us pause here.

If your background is science, or physics, or computer science, you probably realize that the above is a sleuth's version of the Turing Test, which poses this question:

IS HUMANNESS REDUCIBLE TO SQUIGGLES?

Can you decide whether an entity behind a wall is human or AI, simply by asking it questions in writing? And without peeking behind the wall?

If you haven't yet heard of this test, here's a quick recap:

Alan Turing was a certified genius working for British Intelligence's SigInt division at Bletchley Park during WWII. He attained fame for having helped break the German Enigma encryption machine, but also for his early work on computers, chess-playing computer programs, and artificial intelligence. His famous test is about the latter.

And by the way, if this reminds you of Kolmogorov's (restated) question, you are not far wrong. Both questions are about *the information containable in a string of ink squiggles*, although Kolmogorov did not care what the info was about, whereas the Hon. Judge here does.

And just why would it matter to you, as an investor?

QUERYING THE STOCK MARKET THROUGH THE INTERNET TURING SLOT

Because, if you are investing based only on "information" you get from the Internet, you are really communicating with an invisible entity behind your screen, *treating the Internet as a Turing slot.*

The question is: How much can you *really* tell about "info" you get through that convenient slot, that lets you "invest" while sipping coffee?

Like Judge Turing in the above courtroom, you too have no idea who (or what) is behind the Internet info. It could be a benevolent guru who dispenses free and valuable advice, or it may be a slick rascal who tries to sell you electronic tulip bulbs (aka Bitcoin), or even a Russian hacker promoting a nonexistent gold mine, complete with photoshopped photos, expertly faked financial statements, and made-up executive CVs.

So one more time: How can a fable about the Turing Test help you?

THE TURING TEST IS INCONCLUSIVE

Let's get back then to Judge Turing's court-room, to see how that drama was resolved.

You, Mr. Percy Mason, Esq., just spent a whole morning querying the entity behind the wall, first about poetry, then about movie stars, then about accounting, psychology, and the latest baseball scores. It answered all questions perfectly, with just a few human-like mistakes. The judge concluded that you neither proved nor disproved either your respondent's humanity or its AI-ness.

Then the DA had a go, and after an hour, the judge similarly could not conclude who's (or what's) what.

THE DRAMA IS RESOLVED

You are tempted to ask for a mistrial, when your detective, Ms. Sleutzky, who has always been impatient and impulsive, jumps to her feet, runs past the judge's chair, and kicks the wall mightily. The wall crumbles, exposing a room where two men in black suits are tapping at keyboards, while a third is debating with a fourth how best to answer the latest question.

The DA turns pale as his ruse is exposed, and the public gallery erupts in laughter while Judge Turing bangs his gavel. Presently, the judge levies a fine of $1,729 on Ms. Sleutzky (which you happily pay), cancels the DA's law license on the spot, and releases your client with a not guilty verdict.

All's well, it seems, that ends well.

But what are the investment implications of this dramatic ending?

TURING QUESTION IS ANSWERED BY THE CONSTRAINT

First, it's clear that the answer to the famous Turing Test question—whether you can determine if an entity is human or not strictly by querying it in writing—is less relevant than its *constraint*: That *you are not allowed to peek behind the wall.*

And the reason is that *it's impossible to contain the essence of "humanness" in squiggles of ink* on paper (or blips on a screen), whereas all five senses, together with gut sense, just might do it.

Perhaps not with 100% certainty—see Kahneman's "System 1" thinking with its 70-80% hit rate—but certainly better than if done via "System 2" squiggles.

And if we take this into a higher plane—one that Alan Turing probably intended—the question becomes: What does it mean "to be human?" In other words, *can we shoehorn all of "humanness" into categories?* And since commerce, both fear and greed, but also magnanimity and creativity, and productivity and sociability, and all the rest of it, are parts of being human also, the same question applies: *Can we shoehorn commerce completely into ink squiggles*?

And if we cannot (as the test neatly proves), *what then would be left out if we tried?*

VERDICT: THE CORTEX IS GUILTY.

What's left out is the *uncategorizable* part of humanness, the data your cortex threw out as it converted the rest into categories to do "System 2" thinking on: science… logic… math… and accounting and CFA-style stock picking.

Two key questions emerge out of the Turing Test, with relevance to your task of outperforming the market:

First: Where is this left-out data—the Dark Information? Where does it reside, in your brain?

And *Second:* Even if you managed to find it, *how could you access non-categorizable data using a categorizing brain*? (Please remember Jacob Lurie here.)

These two questions, of course, are the keys to the book. Luckily, we have some evidence of how they are handled.

Oddly, though, it's not by humans, but by computers.

CHAPTER 7

CHESS PLAYERS' POINT OF VIEW

Stockfish vs. Leela: forecasting vs. remembering forward.

Yes, *computers who play chess.*

Now, you may ask:

Why look at chess *computers* in a book about *human* sleuth investing?

Well, Warren Buffett once compared investing to battling a smart opponent—"Mr. Market." This opponent is brilliant, but he can also make mistakes. And so it is in the case of you playing a computer at chess. The computer can also be brilliant, but it, too, can make mistakes.

The question is, who will make more mistakes, you, or it?

But (you may ask) aren't the stakes in chess and the market different, money vs. bragging rights?

That is true, but they are not *that* different: Yes, in stocks you are trying to take Mr. Market's money, while he's trying to take yours. However, in chess, your opponent tries to get a piece of your rating, and you're trying to take a piece of his. And in the long run, a higher rating may get you more invitations to tournaments, and—if that's your aim—also help you earn more.

Now what are these ratings?

CHESS RATINGS FAIRLY WON

Every serious chess player has *an Elo rating* (named after the professor who proposed it), measured in *points based on the player's record of wins and losses.*

Just how are these ratings computed?

Say you are a rated chess player. If you win a game, your rating goes up, your opponent's goes down. If at the game's start, your opponent's rating was higher than yours, your win would give you a bigger boost. If your opponent wins, he would get a boost, but a smaller one, because he was stronger to begin with. Same for you, if you were stronger before the match started.

In other words, taking a risk to play a stronger chess player gives you a bigger reward for a higher risk of losing—and an incentive of a smaller penalty. Conversely, a stronger player playing it safe by playing a weaker player gets a smaller reward for a smaller risk of losing, but risks a bigger Elo bite if the other wins.

It's a fair system all around: over time, the strong players' ratings float up, the weak ones' sink.

Thus chess, like the stock market, is democratic. It doesn't matter where you came from, who your parents are, whether you are a man or a woman, or what your social standing is. Chess is a pure mental fight, brain vs. brain, with both you and your opponent able to see the same data, both having the same fair chance.

Or do you?

TWO ANALOGIES OF CHESS TO INVESTING

Let me put forward *two analogies* of investing vs. computerized chess.

In the **first analogy**, the answer to the above question would be **Yes**. The analogy then becomes a pure fight of your brain against a computer playing like a human. Yes, perhaps faster and without (or with fewer) mistakes, but with all info being known to both sides, and both using the same kind of thinking: "System 2."

In the **second analogy**, however, the answer would be **No**, it is not an equal fight, since here the computer would be thinking *unlike* a human, i.e., "System 1," and so would *know what you cannot*, even though both of you see the *same* data. (Forget for the moment the "how.")

So, which is it?

Let's take both analogies in order.

FIRST ANALOGY:

YOUR BRAIN AGAINST A "COMPUTERIZED BRAIN"

Because chess has such precise rules, from early on it was a tempting field for automation. As early as 1948, before computers became powerful, Norbert Wiener, the father of cybernetics, described how a chess program could use a depth-limited search with an Evaluation Function to pick the "best" moves.

Based on his paper, two years later Claude Shannon, the father of (*reductionist*) information theory, described further methods of computer chess. A year after that, none other than Alan Turing, whom Shannon had met (and whose avatar we met in the allegorical courtroom), described a program able to play chess from start to finish, using only a paper-based computation method.

From those humble beginnings, chess-playing computers blossomed, with Shannon's method providing the basis for all early algorithms of machine chess. Each move-choice is seen as a "decision tree" branch, forming a structure of connected move-choices. The tree's "nodes" are the board positions resulting from such choices.

Can this hint at new methods of sleuthing?

Not exactly. But they sure can help you *sift* stocks better, to find the likeliest ones to sleuth. Wait and see.

COMPUTATIONAL EXPLOSION

Even in the early years, automating higher-level playing causes so-called computational explosion: Based on chess-games data, there are on average 36 possible moves per position. An average game lasts 30-40 moves if the game is played to resignation, or around 70 moves if it is played to the bitter/sweet end: mate, draw, or stalemate. Therefore, if you want to compute the best move exhaustively—good luck! After the first move-choice by each player, there are about 400 possible positions, and after two move-choices by each, about 200,000 such. And after three moves, about 120 million.

Why so many?

It is simply a matter of compounding probabilities, when each new move gives birth to so many more probable moves, each of which yields ever more multiplying possibilities. Fairly soon it becomes humanly impossible to consider them all— even for a computer. No matter how fast the computer is, it soon becomes well-nigh impossible for it to consider all possible future positions—and certainly it is impossible to do so in your head. Even grandmasters do not look at much more than about fifty possible moves to find the best one.

And now a question: Which of Kahneman and Tversky's two thinking modes, "System 1" and "System 2," do you think computers use? And which do chess masters use?

BOTH MEN AND (EARLY) CHESS COMPUTERS USE "SYSTEM 2" THINKING

To a very large degree, both use "System 2" thinking—methodical, logical, using *categories*. Each possible move is a category of its own, with quantifiable advantages and disadvantages, and with a player having to decide among them, based solely on the data seen on the chessboard.

Yes indeed. Like CFA investing in stocks by the numbers.

A CFA investor must decide which stock to pick, *based strictly on the numerical financial statements* in print or on screen, using value investing methods. Just like a chess computer manipulating only the board data, the CFA manipulates only the ink squiggles of the financial statements, to arrive at "the best (cheapest) stock pick." By the numbers only. Say lowest price to Net-Net, or lowest EV/EBITDA, or any other ratio.

How is the equivalent done in chess? Either by human or a computer?

Essentially the same way, via "System 2" thinking methods that compare all categories, to see which is best. And, like CFA investing, it's also done "by the numbers."

But which numbers? And how?

How can either a chess computer or a chess master's brain choose which of the fast-exploding possibilities to compare? After all, there are so many! In other words, how to *target* your (or your computer's) chess-move decision-making? On which *portion* of the exploding avalanche of possibilities?

Part of the answer is *memory*.

HUGE MEMORY IS A BIG ADVANTAGE—IN "SYSTEM 2" THINKING

Researchers found that higher-level chess players can recall more similar positions than amateurs in previous games which they have studied, and so they can *focus their thinking* on the more promising moves. Their mode of thinking is still "System 2," but as chess experts, they can also use intuition + memory to focus on positions that had either led to a *win*, or to *material gain*, or to a *positional advantage*. All of which require a few "System 1" quick decisions on *incomplete info*; however, the major decisions still break down into *choices among categories*, i.e., "System 2" thinking.

Which, of course, is how many stock-picking algos operate: Numbers in, Buy/Sell orders out. Their advantage is: No emotions. But what are their flaws?

Or, returning to chess-playing computers in this "System 2 analogy," what don't *they* see?

CHESS, A GAME OF CATEGORIES

Since chess, played by either humans or computers, is almost pure "System 2"—methodical, logical—thinking, that's also how early programs were written to have the computer play chess. And like any program written in ink or bits, whether Turing's paper-based state-machine or a modern supercomputer code, the method is one of categories, just like the chess game itself, and the trick is how to pick the best among them.

In other words, methodical chess is a *game of two-level search*, first picking the likeliest-best categories to choose *from*, and then, from these, picking the *final* actual move.

Just like CFAs picking stocks, yes. There, the categories are assets and liabilities, balance sheet, income statement, cash flow statements, and all other accounting items you learn in the CFA courses (or the CA designation). You manipulate these numbers to get the "best stock to buy." Either by hand, or via an "algo" based on Pacioli's accounting categories, and perhaps price action in the market—yes, more categories.

What are the equivalent categories in chess?

There are of course many such, because of the exponential explosion, but they can be parsed rationally too, just like Pacioli (an enthusiastic chess-player too) has parsed his accounting.

CATEGORIES OF CHESS—AND SUB-CATEGORIES

First off, there are the three semi-arbitrary categories of *the stage* of the game: the **opening game**, the **middle game**, and an **end game**, each of which with many sub-categories.

For example, in the Opening category alone there are thousands of known openings, most with a name of their own, with variations and sub-variations in each, most of these with names also. Like the Ruy Lopez, the Italian Game, the Sicilian Defense, the French Defense, the Caro-Kann Defense, the Queen's gambit, the King's Indian... Or the more modern ones like the Reti Opening, or the Ruy Lopez-Berlin Defense, the Najdorf Sicilian... And many more.

Naturally no chess player can study them all, but most serious players do learn the main openings—between 80 and 100—memorizing the best "lines" in each and the traps to avoid. Equally obvious, many thousands of chess openings *can* be stored in a file that a computer can access fast, giving the machine an obvious advantage there over a human brain.

The same also goes for end games, with a file of their own. As for the middle game, here anything goes. Or rather, *almost* anything. Because there are rules that hint at what is *usually* best in the middle game. These are called *heuristics*, or "rules of thumb," and are based on experience, enabling the player (or the computer) to make moves with higher likelihood of success, even without onerous computation.

Here, for example, are a few such heuristics:

CHESS' PRACTICAL RULES OF THUMB

Control the center of the board, develop your pieces quickly, move knights before bishops, avoid moving the same piece twice, don't bring out the queen too early, castle before the tenth move, connect rooks, keep the knights centered (aka "knights on the rim are dim"), avoid doubled pawns, and many more such.

What would be equivalent heuristics in CFA investing? (Sticking to numbers and categories.)

For example: Don't buy high P/E stocks, no IPOs, no stocks without dividends, no trading, never buy a stock unless you are willing to hold it for 5–10 years (Buffett says the ideal is "forever"). No stock with excessive debt. I'm sure you can find more.

Back to chess:

Because so many possible board situations exist, a chess player (or a computer) who knows how to identify *which* situation he or she (or it) is facing—i.e., what is its category—has an advantage.

Stated differently: the first task in advanced chess playing is to *identify the category* into which the situation falls, and *name* it, then *retrieve from memory* which moves come out best.

Sound familiar?

CHESS PLAYING DOVETAILS THE CORTEX'S MODUS OPERANDI

Of course. It is what your cortex does, when one of its columnar neurons flows the sensory data through its "vertical neural net," and reduces it to categories via the Mountcastle algorithm. Only then can the brain search through its memory—likely in the hippocampus, but perhaps also distributed in the "brain cloud"—and do "System 2" thinking on the recently produced categories. That way, it can come up with a judgment of which choice is best, or which forecast is likeliest, or even how urgent is the task—in chess it's because the clock has almost run down.

But because possible chess responses are so impossibly numerous, your brain *must* use heuristics, like the ones above. And, since humans play chess via "System 2" thinking, the first chess-playing programs naturally were written to imitate what humans do—see the work of Wiener, Shannon, and Turing (listed in the recommended books list at the back.) They are all pure "System 2" thinking. That is: identify the category, use math / "System 2" to compare various categories, and finally choose the best one.

Hmmm...

Doesn't this, too, remind you of the problem of stock-picking, to find the best stock out of the tens of thousands presented to you daily by Mr. Market?

You are not far wrong. These two problems are somewhat similar—but *only somewhat*, since the number of choices in the market are finite (though the "rules" are far less predictable than in chess), whereas the total number of moves in chess is impossibly large, so *neither* a human brain *nor* a computer can search them all.

HOW TO NARROW THE FIELD OF SEARCH

So how to do it?

Assume you want to find a specific target hiding among an impossibly large crowd. You can't move your gun in micro-amounts over the entire "field of fire," searching for the target based on fitness criteria, because the field is so wide. You must first pre-point the gun approximately, before micro-adjusting the search. Your first challenge, then, is: *How to reduce the number of categories/moves, into a subset* small enough, on which the computer program (or your brain, if you are a grandmaster) can use System-2 final-picking search?

But be careful, now! This initial sifting can make your search *faster and better*, avoiding time wasted on bad choices. However, it can also make it *faster and worse*, if you inadvertently threw out the best move! This is especially so in the case of human (or human-like) thinking. Since the very process of categorization (as per Naftali Tishby's findings) throws out the uncategorized (or uncategorizable) data—among which the best move may just be hiding.

So: How can you do more of the *good* sifting, and avoid the *bad* kind?

MISSING MULTI-BAGGERS VS. LOSING MONEY

Once again this is similar to the problem of stock picking: How to ensure that you don't lose that rare hundred-bagger that can make your fortune, by restricting the criteria of choice *too* much?

Let's see now: How is it done in chess?

A "state of the board" is called a ply. A "move" is two plies—one by each player. Each ply's move-choice leads to many possible future plies, each initiated by the player whose turn it is to move. Some moves are forced—e.g., by the need to get out of "check," while others are impossible (aka "pins"), like exposing the king to check, or highly ill-advised (e.g., exposing the queen). However, most moves are a matter of choice. The question is: How to compare these choices, if you must consider an impossibly large future tree of possible moves?

The computer's way to compare possible moves—remember, we are still in "System 2"—is via what is called an *Evaluation Function*, or EF.

EVALUATION FUNCTION MAKES THE CHOICE. BUT WHO MAKES THE EF?

There's an EF in stocks too, you know.

If you are a CFA (but not a sleuth), you seek value via an Evaluation Function that lets you choose the best stock based on some parameter.

Unlike chess, though, in stock picking this Evaluation Function usually has a single parameter. For example, low P/E, low Price/BV, low Price/WC, or any other single criterion. Only in rare cases does it have two. For example, in Joel Greenblatt's Magic Formula: first you choose stocks with highest Return on Capital, and out of these, you choose those with the highest EBIT/EV (see glossary). Or, in yet another method, you first choose stocks with the highest growth, then the one with the lowest P/E among them.

Note, though, that in either of the above, the two parameters are *sequential*, not a *combined* function. *First* highest Return on Capital bunch, *then* higher EBIT/EV of these.

In chess, per contra, the EF contains several categories/variables, *all used at once*, not one after the other.

CHESS' EVALUATION FUNCTION HAS SIX PARAMETERS

Here is the typical list of categories used in computer chess: material, mobility, king safety, center control, pawn structure, and, occasionally, something called king tropism.

You can look up in any search engine how each category is calculated, but briefly: **Material** is the sum of values of all pieces and pawns of each player. (See below for value numbers.) **Mobility** is roughly the number of legal moves available to a player. **King safety** is a set of bonuses and penalties for the location of the king and the pawns and pieces close to it. **Center control** is how many pawns and pieces occupy or project on the four center spaces. **Pawn structure** is a set of penalties and bonuses for strengths and weaknesses in pawn structure. **King tropism** is a bonus for closeness (or penalty for distance) of certain pieces to the opposing king.

The key is: Each of the above can be precisely calculated. (So, in theory, you can even compute it by hand—as indeed Turing had done several times, each move taking half an hour…)

To arrive at a ply's EF value for each player, each of the above terms is multiplied by a different factor, and the results summed up. The EF is measured in centi-pawns, when each pawn is worth 1. For reference, the queen is worth 9, knights and bishops 3 each, rooks 5, and kings are considered worth 200, since nothing can make up for a king's loss. (You can look up other methods of valuing each piece.)

Once the computer has computed the EF "value" of the current "ply", it can look at the *main* possible moves (assuming the other side will respond with *its* best move), then compare future EFs based on this particular current move, and make its choice.

HOW FAR AHEAD CAN WE SEE IN CHESS?

The recurring computer-chess question is, *how far into the future can it look*?

The answer: If we go by brute force, as far as its memory and microchip speeds will allow. But because of the computational explosion, the computer must make *some* sifting decisions on where to *focus* its effort.

But focus how?

Even the early chess computers had a large library of openings, an equally large one for endgames, and as many heuristics as possible for the middle game. Thus, these early chess-playing programs could evaluate the EF of each "ply" based on possible best-moves following it—and the best moves following that—and those after, so as to maximize the value of future chain-of-plies. Thus, each stored opening and endgame already saved some sifting effort, by assuming each side will do its best, maximizing gain while minimizing risk.

This, essentially, is the minimax strategy, one of the basics of general game theory.

SEARCH DICTATES HOW FAR WE CAN LOOK

Most chess computers do it this way to this day. Even "Deep Blue," the famous computer that beat Kasparov, does it like this, as do most of its commercial progeny now being sold as "computer engines" on which players can train and search for "best moves:" Fritz, Stockfish, Rybka, as well as Magnus, the chess program sold by the current world champion.

Most of these computers can play at master level, some even grandmaster, and a few even beat the best human players. But to all intents and purposes, these chess-playing computers have been, and still are, *categorizers*. They are, essentially, *an attempt to copy "System 2" human thinking in silicon.*

Yes: Just like a computerized stock-picking algorithm using Compustat databases tries to imitate how a CFA picks stocks using only the financial statements.

See again Jim O'Shaughnessy's methods, Joel Greenblatt's Magic Formula, Ben Graham's value picks, or any of the freely available "screens" based on financials. That, in essence, is also how most computers play chess. By the numbers only.

Or rather, *played.*

Because all this "System 2" stuff is in the past:

SECOND ANALOGY:

CHESS-PLAYING COMPUTERS BEHAVING LIKE THOUSAND-YEAR-OLD SLEUTHS

Just as modern investing is slowly turning into sleuthing, so have modern chess-playing computers turned into "System 1" "thinkers," who use deep-learning Neural Nets to make their move-decisions. And once they began, there was no going back.

For example, Alpha Zero, one of the first Neural Net-based chess programs, beat Stockfish, the top ranked first-generation computer, 28-0, with 72 draws, in a 100-game match.

Later, Neural Net-based computers could do even better. And it is in these latest machines' mode of operation that we can find the answers to the question posed before, about the Big Prize this book is after: *Where is the Dark Info (that-cannot-be-named) hiding, and how to access it?*

But before we go there, let's pause for a moment, to see whether we can learn to invest better—or just target our sleuthing better—even from these early, first-generation, "System 2" chess-playing machines.

Can we?

MULTI-FACTOR EVALUATION FUNCTIONS FOR STOCK SIFTING

We sure can.

The early computer chess programs all used Evaluation Functions with several parameters, while CFA-type investing uses mostly *one-parameter* EF to find value, or at best three.

So can we perhaps take a page from these *early* chess-playing computers, and look for *multi-factor Evaluation Functions for stocks*, too?

Yes we can. However, please beware: these stock EFs should *not* be used for blind-picking Buys and Sells, but *rather as "sifters"* of the large universe of stocks, to reduce the many thousands of stocks into a few likely picks, *on which to do deep sleuthing*, since sleuthing is so intense and time consuming.

And, as usual, before setting out to design a model, it's best to begin with a conceptual approach. Here is one I've found most useful.

THREE MAIN PARAMETERS FOR A STOCK'S EVALUATION FUNCTION (EF)

The following three parameters can often capture much of the essential qualities of superior companies:

1. **Business quality**, measured via the Return on Equity (or Return on Capital, your choice),
2. **Management quality**, measured via the gross margins, and
3. the company's **Market quality**, indicated by the sales growth.

You are welcome to choose other parameters, if you wish, but I found that these ones work well. The reason is simple: The best companies have fast revenue growth, good management that drops most of the revenue to the bottom line, and that does it with very little capital. So when combined, these produce two powerful sifting indicators that capture much of a company's excellence, to help you ensure you don't waste your precious sleuthing time.

SIFTING INDICATORS

A. COMPANY'S QUALITY INDICATOR: Q

Each of these parameters is measured in percent. And with all three falling in the range of approx. 0% to 100% (few negative, few above 100%), simply summing them all up (i.e., equal weights to all) gives a useful EF, the *company's* quality indicator, which for ease of memory we can call **Q**. The higher its value, the higher the company's quality.

Or, in math: Q = RoE+GM+SlsGr. Anything above 80 is worth attention. Anything above 100 is worth a lot of attention. Another above 120 is worth a big chunk of your sleuthing time.

(By the way: I found that a company's Q often captures much of Warren and Charlie's concepts of "moat" and "franchise," via the result produced by this EF.)

B. STOCK'S VALUE INDICATOR: V

A second indicator would show if the stock price of a high Q company is cheap enough today to spend sleuthing time on. In effect, this second indicator measures *how many "units-of-quality" you are buying per "price-multiple unit,"* which is a distant cousin of the Growth at a Reasonable price (GARP) Evaluation Function.

This second indicator, the *stock's* value indicator, we can simply call V. It is computed this way:

V = Q/(EV/EBITDA)

Anything above 2 is interesting, above 4 is fascinating, and above 5 almost compelling.

But remember: these two EFs are *not* Buy/Sell triggers, but a "Maybe/maybe-not-worth-sleuthing" sifter.

Look up Appendix 1 for a list of 15 companies with both high Q and V values.

Back to chess, then.

What about the *modern* chess-playing computers? What do they do differently? And in what way can it give you the key for what I've called the "Dark Info" of investing? The kind that cannot be named?

NEXT-GENERATION CHESS-PLAYING COMPUTERS REALLY DO IT DIFFERENTLY

This way: Modern chess-playing computers have *abandoned "System 2" "thinking," and use only "System 1,"* so as to generate their *own* huge library of heuristics, where each past move of every past ply is seen separately. This way, *each future pick is made as if the computer is acting on instinct—yes, like a sleuth*—but one whose precision you cannot (yet) imitate.

Yes, just as you'd like to be able to do, when picking stocks. So how do these second-generation chess computers do it?

The two "System 1" chess-playing computers I am talking about are Leela and Alpha Zero. Or, to be precise, they are not just computers, but are really giant Neural Networks.

What are these?

A short segue is again in order.

NEURAL NETS, THE ANTIDOTE TO "SYSTEM 2" THINKING

In 1969, Marvin Minsky wrote (together with Seymour Papert) a seminal book called *Perceptrons*. In the book, (inter alia) he proved that an electronic neural network with a single front layer that received an input, and a single back layer that generated an output, was limited in its ability to "learn:" i.e., identify new inputs. Some logical operations (an XOR gate, or the "Exclusive Or," if you want to know) the Perceptron could not do. The proof was impeccable, and so, for thirty years, few bothered building fancier NNs or teaching them stuff. For this, many blamed Minsky (unjustly in my opinion). But finally, in 1986, Geoff Hinton (some of whose lectures I later audited), David Rumelhart and Ronald J. Williams published a paper suggesting that, maybe, by inserting a middle layer or two between the front and the back ones, the NN could bypass the limitation. Could it?

MIDDLE LAYERS ENABLE BACK-PROPAGATION—AND LEARNING

It sure could. Because unlike the AND and OR gates, an XOR gate did require an intermediate hidden layer, for feedback. This nifty trick became known as *back-propagation*, which basically was assigning weights to the internal nodes via repeated trial and error, with feedback going as it should, backwards. As in democracy when those below tell those above where they (the above) went wrong, and so they'd better change, if they want better results for everyone. Now, with propagation done backwards and forward via the mid-layers (often more than just one), the NN could much better "generalize" the "meaning" of the mish-mash input data, and so "learn" what "generally" "led to" what.

Forget for a moment the parts of "led to" and "meaning," and just focus on "generalize." But because many refused to, for years insisting on *causality* (i.e., "led to") and a *meaning* (i.e., a "greater significance"), it took fifty years (after the Perceptron) for another top-notch NN scientist, Naftali Tishby of Hebrew University (together with Fernando Pereira and William Bialek) to find (in 2019), what *really* went on *inside* the NN during the learning.

Which was also the moment something clicked in my brain, and I decided to write this book.

INFORMATION BOTTLENECK AND SELECTIVE FORGETTING

What Tishby and his collaborators found they named "information bottleneck," which in my humble opinion doesn't really capture the full import of their stupendous discovery. To cut to the chase, "learning" appeared to be nothing less than the process of

1. *categorizing* the mish-mash of data entering the Net by *dividing it into (invented) categories,*
2. giving *names* (or addresses) to these invented categories,
3. *assigning* parts of the mish-mash data to individual *categories-silos*, then
4. ***throwing away*** all data points that could *not* be categorized.

This was a truly momentous discovery, as Geoff Hinton himself later affirmed. And it was momentous because (in Tishby's words), it showed that ***forgetting* (*the uncategorized*), *is part of learning*.**

And, almost as an aside, this discovery also proved two more momentous things.

TWO MORE KEY DISCOVERIES

First, that *categories do not come from nature*. They may, but we have no way of knowing this. What is clear is that a Neural Net—and a human brain too, as per Jeff Hawkins' work— divides its mish-mash input into *categories of its own invention*. Whether these are equal to nature's categories is unknown and perhaps unknowable (which is, of course, the reductionism question).

But **second,** and perhaps most important, **is that some of the data that enters the NN**—and also the brain, where the cortex's six layers are composed of them—**is thrown away so as to be able to forecast and do "System 2" thinking, and logic, and science—and yes, CFA investing too**. And ***this thrown-off data can be tracked.***

Let me repeat, so you don't miss the full import of this last part to you as a sleuth-investor:

Your cortex, in order to learn, throws away some of what goes into it, including the fruit of your sleuthing research. And it does this, so as to be able to "understand," i.e., "generalize" the rest, and so make buy and sell decisions, *CFA-style.*

And, of course, so do the brains of your opponents, the (underperforming) CFAs, whose money you aim to take.

DISCARDED DARK INFO IS THE HIDDEN TREASURE

The obvious questions are:

Where does the mish-mash's *discarded* Dark Info go? And does it contain any *useful* info, even though it's *uncategorizable*? And if so, can you access it while CFAs cannot? And if so, how?

As you'll see below, chess computers definitely do it— the latest kind that use NNs, that is—so it's worthwhile to see how, then perhaps you could learn how to do it too.

But before we leave the topic, let's make sure (briefly) we don't gloss over the comparison of the brain to a Neural Net: it shouldn't be taken as a given. Neural Nets are electronic constructs, while your brain is organic. Can the two really be similar?

THE BRAIN AS YOUR MAIN INVESTMENT TOOL

First off, which part of "the brain" are we talking about? Because the brain is not homogeneous, you know. It has several parts, some of them practically ancient, like the brain stem, but others evolved much more recently, like the cortex. The older parts are different from each other, because it took a long time for them to evolve, and so they developed specialties that enable each to serve different functions. But the cortex, the newest part, is the same almost all the way through. It has six layers, which are composed almost exclusively of columns of neurons perpendicular to the layers, going from outside to inside. And all these columns are practically the same no matter their task: whether handling hearing, sight, touch, motor functions, or forecasting, *they all use the same algorithm*, called the Mountcastle algorithm, named after Vernon Mountcastle, who discovered it. That, by the way, was also a momentous thing, because this algo's biological Neural Net is key to the brain's operation. "System 2" operation, that is.

YOUR CATEGORIZER CORTEX DISCARDS SOME KEY INFO

Each neuron in the cortex's vertical column's Neural Net amplifies some signals, mutes others, and connects to other nets of neurons so as to "generalize" the brain's understanding of what goes on. Same as a back-propagating NN does. Eric Kendal got the Nobel prize for finding some of the amplification and muting process, and other scientists added to the knowledge since. But in simple words, *the cortex is a categorizer*. It takes a mish-mash of sensory data, both from your body's external five senses and a bunch of inside sensors, like weight, pain, fear and euphoria, and others to which there is no name and so they remain biological/physical only, and converts the entire mish-mash to categories. On these categories, the **cortex does an enormous amount of *ongoing* forecasting of what should come next**, then compares these forecasts to what *really* happens, and if it's different, it issues an alert.

Like what kind of alert?

Like your foot not meeting an expected stair at the right-forecasted time, because it (the stair) had been broken, and so your brain (or rather your spine, which has a lot of neurons too) issues an urgent order to your hands to grab the rails, just in case. Or your hand not finding the door key on the customary hook, and seeing broken glass on the floor, makes you reach for the baseball bat, just in case.

That is: your brain does an ongoing categorizing (in the cortex) and forecasting (ditto), *discarding (into somewhere) what it can't categorize*, compares (in "System 2") its forecasts to what really goes on, then issues orders (usually in "System 1") after a "System 2" forecast/alert.

So again, how to find where the discarded data went? Because, obviously, there is your advantage.

Since you are getting impatient, I can tell you that very soon you'll hear the story of Lady Gaga and Tony Bennett, for which you'll need a hankie or a Kleenex box, and there you'll very likely find the answer. But for now, back to Neural Nets and the spectacularly new kind of "System 1" chess that they play, and one more actual case study for you with *practical* sleuthing techniques.

THE FIRST CHESS-PLAYING COMPUTERS USING "SYSTEM 1" THINKING

Unlike IBM's Watson and Deep Blue, those first "System-2" thinking computers that were designed for a specific task (Jeopardy and chess, respectively), Alpha Zero and Leela were not pre-programmed with libraries and heuristics and EFs. Instead, they *learned from their own experience*, by using a deep-learning Neural Network that *draws meaning out of the game data all on its own*. These programs used *no* named openings, *no* middle games, *no* end games, *no* rules of thumb, *no* libraries, *no* pre-loaded heuristics. Just playing, and remembering.

But what were these programs fed with, to start?

Only the chess rules: how each piece moves, what's a check, what's a mate, and so on. No values of pieces, no heuristics, no libraries. The program was then told to simply go and play—play against a copy of itself, that is. Again, and again, and again.

And again.

And of course, they kept track of everything they did, every ply, every move, every win, every loss, every draw. Everything.

ANTI-REDUCTIONISM: REMEMBERING TOTAL STATES

However, the program did *not* remember in categories. Just *the total picture of every ply*, and what actual move the program decided on, in that particular game.

And it remembered what was the *ultimate* result of *that* game: *Was this move or a similar one, in this ply or a similar one, associated with a final win, a loss, or a draw? And out of the total number of games played, what was the percentage?*

That was it. (But see below what "similar" meant, or rather didn't.)

For example: by January 2022, the program called Leela Chess Zero had *played over half a billion games against a copy of itself*, at the rate of about *1 million games a day*. This enormous playing experience made it the equivalent of a stupendously old chess sleuth, *with perfect memory of half a billion actual physical games* played over thousands of years—a virtual player that can recollect every ply, every move, and—this is key—*<u>the probability of win</u> associated with each move, in <u>percent</u>.*

FROM "SYSTEM 2" THINKING TO "SYSTEM 1"

Again: not games broken into categories, with EF value-numbers, but the *<u>actual</u> record of winning of each move*, based on Leela's hugely long "past." Not categories.

It was this part that yanked the modern chess-playing computer out of the realm of "System 2" thinking-in-categories into "System 1" (instinctive) thinking. The chess computer no longer had to compare the *numerical* value of each *potential* move's EF to *other* moves' EFs, nor to *sift-down* the millions of potential moves into a manageable subset of moves.

No. Instead, *each move came with a record of success that showed its value*—in that particular ply, or a similar ply—*to the game's goal*, as proven over half a billion games. In percentages.

But similar *how*? How to define "similarity?"

There was no need to tell Leela how to judge this. The Neural Net just tried this and that, and over time, kept what worked best. Over half a billion games, it soon approached the real best.

Why it worked? Leela didn't care a bit about that. Only that it *did.*

Leela's program did *not* need to break each ply into six categories, and turn the six-pack into an EF number. Instead, *each move in a specific ply was a category of its own*, a sui generis, that *came with its own long-term, multi-lifetime performance record.* So Leela's decision plan was easy-peasy: the program simply had to go from best historical move (in %) of this ply to best historical move next ply to the best in the next, with "best" defined as "what had *already* succeeded over the last half a billion games."

During the first hundreds of thousands of games, this "success" percentage was still rough, but as Leela played more and more, the percentage became more and more accurate. Even after a few hundred million games, this "best" was continually updated, although minimally, as the machine played more and more games.

"SYSTEM 1" CHESS NO LONGER MATERIALISTIC

One fascinating result was *that because there was no EF, there was no emphasis on material*, and so Leela could sacrifice pieces easily for strategic advantage, or for precise tactical targeted bombing so far in the future that no "System 2" could see it coming. Indeed, often a minor, incomprehensible pawn move in an early ply would later be seen as eerily prophetic more than thirty moves later. In other words, when Leela was really sure, it didn't care for occasional material losses, and held on to a position everyone else thought foolish.

Remind you of investing?

Yup. When you are really and truly sure of your stock position, ironclad sure, when you know so much more about the company than everyone else, *physically* know, then you can hold on to a stock through deep drawdowns that would panic 99% of CFAs, because they don't know what you know, physically, until the stock becomes the rare hundred-bagger that they all miss.

Or hold on to shorts, too. Like when you know that the CEO of Small Conglomerate is on the way out, and his inexperienced CFO will come in, and have to deal with the offshore mess.

Or, like knowing what IBM's people really thought of their CEO and chairman.

If you know the 99.9% likely result, on a *physical* level, you can then ignore all other info expressed in squiggles. Only by having *physical* information to which all other players are blind, info which you can get only by sleuthing, and "System 1" instinctive thinking. Based on physical actualities. Not inky traces, but the physical events themselves, sui generis.

And so it was for Leela: there was no need for *pre-sifting* of categories, no comparing EFs, no categorizing. Just delving into a thousand-year-old memory of this chess-playing Methuselah, *who then just did what "felt right" to it*, based on its own half-a-billion-games physical experience, which it kept correcting and updating.

No need to look far into the imagined future. Look instead into the *actual* physical past. Its own.

Alright (I hear you saying), so it *is* possible to do this with modern chess-playing computers. But can *humans* do it?

Apparently some already do.

Grandmaster Mikhail Tal (aka "The Magician from Riga") was once asked: How many moves ahead do you look at, when you plan your next move?

His answer? None.

He may have been joking, of course, but most probably not.

Wouldn't you like to do this, too, when you invest?

LEELA'S METHOD FOLLOWS CHARLIE MUNGER'S RECOMMENDATION, OR RATHER LKY'S

You could, or at least aim towards it and improve in time, as this book's last chapter will show you. But first we must put the idea in explicit, current context:

What Leela did, actually follows what Charlie Munger recommends as the best rule of success in anything: in investing, career, life, anything at all. He calls it the Lee Kuan Yew rule.

This rule has two parts:

1. See what works, and do *more* of it.

2. See what doesn't work, and do *less* of it, or preferably *none.*

THE LEE KUAN YEW RULE

Charlie Munger attributes this rule to Lee Kuan Yew, the founder of modern Singapore. LKY insists modestly that this is how he had built his city state. And, as you'll see, this rule underlies the last chapter of this book—but with one slight but very important modification:

Do more of what works for ***you****, and don't do what doesn't work for* ***you****.*

Not in general, not for everyone. But for you.

AND YES, IT IS EVOLUTION'S RULE, TOO

The biologists among you (I am sure there are some) have probably realized that Leela's and Alpha Zero's method (and LKY's) is really natural evolution's method, the one Darwin discovered. And it is also, incidentally, also how Neural Networks learn. They try placing a bit of data into this (invented) category, then into another one, track what works (i.e., forecasts) and amplify that connection, but if it doesn't work, the NN weakens it so it won't be used again. Just as Eric Kendal found how human brain neurons operate.

Yes. Brain, Neural Nets, evolution, it is all of a piece.

Similarly, these electronic chess-playing Methuselahs also try this and that move over half a billion games, keep what works, and throw out what doesn't. Which is why such a method is often referred to as "genetic algorithm." Because similarly, over half a billion years, an organism tries this and that and perhaps a bit of the other, then it (or rather its genetic DNA) retains whatever has worked in this ply (aka "generation"), and goes on to the next ply. And again, and again. And again.

Evolution, too, is a game of "Let's see what survives then make more of it, and let's allow what doesn't work to die, and make less (or none) of it." There is no Evaluation Function in biology, except the Big One: survival, based on *this* specific environment.

Seen this way, the game of chess can be seen as a short "game of king's survival," as *observed and recorded* by (say) Leela's NN, in the environment of chess rules. Or Shogi rules, the Japanese chess. Whatever move(s) had worked in the last games have a better chance (no more than that) of survival in future games. There are no categories. Only plies, and moves, and a slow, overarching, moving finger that writes, and having written, moves on—and becomes better for having observed and written and survived.

Wouldn't you like to invest like this? You can, you know. Just wait for the last chapter. But back to NN-chess for now.

A TOTALLY DIFFERENT KIND OF CHESS

As it learned to play using the above simple rule, Leela was producing a totally different kind of chess-play. It no longer considered openings or endgames, and it kept no record of when knights are best and when doubled pawns are bad, nor any other *generalizations.*

Remember: *generalizations* is what Neural Networks (either electronic, or the Mountcastle Algo in your cortex) do when they convert mish-mash data into *categories.* Leela needed none given to her in advance, as her predecessors had, and so didn't need to forget anything in order to learn. It kept it all, as a record of entire plies as states. How to decide which ply in memory "resembles" the current one? The program *didn't bother about defining the problem, or the category.* It just tried first this, then that, and settled on what worked best over time.

Why it worked? Who cares?

Leela didn't.

She, or rather it, is not a scientist, but a warrior fighting for survival—just as you are in the market.

Leela's plies were *not* broken into categories so as to evaluate their EF numerically. Rather, *each ply was a category all its own.*

Yes, just like a "Kolmogorov random string," without a categorizable order, is a sui generis. A Kantian *ding-am-sich,* a thing in itself. That's how Leela (and Alpha Zero) came to learn how to play, and beat their opponents—which at the beginning was only a mirror program of itself. But then Leela played with other, earlier computer chess-playing programs, Categorizers all, and it beat them too, hands down. And then a cousin of Alpha Zero—AlphaGo—played Go against its twin a few hundred million games (it took one afternoon), and triumphed over the human world Go champ. (And also, by the way, invented a sensational new kind of move.)

LEAVING PLATO'S CAVE

How did Leela do it?

Essentially by abandoning the brain's method of apprehending the world by categorizing it first. *The NN computer, in effect, had left Plato's cave.* It somehow connected with the entire, original, multifarious stream of data from the outside, by going over it again, and again, and again, trying first this, then that, all the time *keeping a record of what worked and what didn't.*

Only that.

It then observed which pattern on the wall followed which preceding patterns, and how much "success" was associated with each of these. In effect, *instead of breaking the Turing wall, it broke the slot, and got all the outside data directly, without converting it into squiggles first.*

LIKE ALICE'S WHITE QUEEN, LEELA REMEMBERS BOTH BACKWARD AND FORWARD

And because of that, we can say that Leela remembered *in detail* backward a huge number of *possible* worlds, then used the success percentages *to forecast the future.* And by so remembering everything backwards, without categories, it could now remember *forward,* too, in *percentages.*

Like *Alice's Adventures in Wonderland,* where the White Queen's memory works forwards too.

"I'm sure mine only works one way," says Alice. "I can't remember things before they happen."

"It's a poor sort of memory that only works backwards," the Queen remarks.

She's of course right. Alice's memory is the kind that older categorizing chess computers used, like Deep Blue. The Queen's memory is like Leela's. *It remembers not in numbers, as in classical physics, but in probabilities, as in modern, quantum physics.*

Who needs quantum computers when you are a White Queen, or Leela, and can do *this*?

A CAVEAT: THE ABOVE ISN'T COMPUTER SCIENCE, JUST AN APPROXIMATION

Now, a caveat: the above is only a rough generalization (yup) of how Alpha Zero and Leela work, with many details omitted and others told in a non-mathematical way. But in general (yup again), that's the way it works. A computer learning the game by playing against itself, and so learning the rules by implication, implicitly, not explicitly.

Just as you are learning sleuthing in this book, yes.

And, before we go to the next chapter, here is a case study that portrays just how you can imitate what Leela does.

CASE HISTORY: DOING WHAT WORKS, NOT DOING WHAT DOESN'T

SELLING WATCHES VIA THE LKY/LEELA METHOD

Here is a story I got from a close family member who once worked for a well-known consulting company. Among his colleagues was a young guy who came from India with little besides a math degree. Let's call this guy Jay. Once arrived in NYC, Jay found work as a salesman in one of those shops that sell seemingly expensive watches to status seekers on a budget. The way it worked, the shop owner explained, a salesman ate what he killed. There was no salary, only a percent of the sales price of the watch he'd sold. The more he sold, the higher the percentage rose. Anything below a certain level of sales, commission was 10%. Anything above that level, 15%, then 20% of any sales above the second threshold, and 25% of anything above that.

WATCHING AND TAKING NOTES OF ACTIONS—AND THEIR RESULTS

No one ever got to 25%, the owner told him, except one woman who sold a lot, because clients only watched her bosoms rather than the watches, so they didn't even notice the price. She earned so much that the owner, to save money, married her. Now no one made 25%; yet Jay, young and ambitious, aspired to. But how to get there? He did not have the boss's wife's attributes, nor any previous sales ability. He therefore began to watch what other salesmen did and took mental notes, which on his lunch break he wrote down in a small copybook in Hindi, then after work, summed up at home, in English, filling up pages—because there was a lot of salesmanship to see.

For example, some salesmen talked a lot, others talked little and listened more. A few did both, but in different proportions. Some salesmen talked about the watch, others about potential impressions of the watch on the buyer's friends, other salesmen still, about sports, and few, very few, asked the customer questions. Some salesmen displayed several watches simultaneously, others brought out watches one by one. Of the latter, some brought the cheap watches first, others the expensive ones. Each salesman had his own technique, except for some who seemed to have no method. These Jay ignored, because he could not learn from them.

CORRELATION IMPORTANT, CAUSATION ISN'T

Obviously, Jay also noted how many watches each of the salesmen sold, and by the type of the watches sold he evaluated approximately how much their sales were in total. Then at home he wrote it all down, and tried to correlate the salesmen's results to what they did or didn't do. But he had to do it very carefully, because he didn't want others to see he was watching them, and also because after a month he was already at 15% commission level. Whatever he was doing, watching and copying the most effective techniques, avoiding the ineffective ones, was somehow working. Even though he had never sold anything before in his life, and all he was doing was copying the actions of others, selectively.

SUCCESS, AND PLATEAU

For the next two months Jay stuck at the 15% commission level, and no matter what he did, he could go no higher. He had apparently exhausted the information content in the others' techniques. Nevertheless, the boss complimented him on his productivity and noted that only the most seasoned salesmen got to 15%, and only after a year, and only very few stayed at that level for more than a month or two, most falling down back to 10% when they lost their edge, whatever that was. Or was it luck?

Jay agreed with the boss that it probably was. However, unlike others, he stayed at 15% and did not slide back, but he still wanted more. The question was, what fresh tricks could he try? Maybe he'd just pick new different methods at random? After all, the cost of trying was low. That is: he would not be penalized, so long as he kept to polite manners. At worst he'd go down in commission temporarily, but he could always go back to what had worked for him before, because he knew exactly what it was.

EXPERIMENTING WITH FURTHER FACTORS—WHILE STILL IGNORING CAUSATION

So Jay began to experiment in what seemed only peripherally connected to sales. For example, one week he displayed the watch on his own wrist, wearing a fine shirt with cufflinks, instead of putting it on the counter, or holding it up. The next week he wore just a shirt, without cufflinks. The first seemed to work better, and two weeks later Jay went to the top of the 15% sales range, close to the next level, but still not in. So he tried a few more variations. First showing the watch front first, then the back, with the company's fancy (often fake) imprint, then doing it in reverse order. Then he also highlighted the watchstrap, not just the watch, then both.

Finally on a whim, he began to track the time of day he was presenting the watch to customers (95% of them men) and began to vary his mode of presentation—both learned from others, and his own refinements. Sometimes he would do this by dropping one trick and trying another, tracking results all the time, and analyzing them at home.

A COMBINATION OF FACTORS HAS A BIGGER IMPACT

Within a month Jay's sales mushroomed, and he was at 20% commission. What was it exactly that worked? To what could he *attribute* his success? He could not tell. It was not any one trick that seemed to matter, but several together did. How to find out which? For a week Jay toyed with the idea of putting all the info into a regression model, and computing "t" statistics and "R square," as he'd learned in his university days in Pune, but he dropped the idea as silly. Using regression on what essentially was human interaction, he felt, was leaving the main item out of it: the two persons interacting, each with a different personality. How could one model that?

As a solid 20 percenter, for the next two months Jay found other salesmen watching him intently, trying to imitate any of his methods they could visibly identify. Two even tried to imitate his Pune accent, which he found funny, but kept his thoughts to himself. Perhaps it was the accent, or maybe other imitations, but some other salesmen succeeded in selling more, and during the next two months the entire store's sales rose significantly. The boss realized that Jay was good for business and suggested making him assistant manager, on a fixed salary plus some commission. But Jay politely declined. Watch sales was not a career for him, only a money-making occupation, and a preparation for a life of something else.

MODIFYING FACTORS BASED ON THE ENVIRONMENT

It was on his fourth month in the store that Jay found that one thing stood out, something he had never noted, and this was: he could vary his own behaviour, depending on the customer's personality or behavior. In other words, customers were not uniform.

For example, he noted that 10% of the customers were left-handed. For these he presented the watch on his own left wrist. Sales to these lefties soared to more than half of presentations. (By that time, he was tracking the success ratio of each sales effort, in percentages, both in general, to check his improvement, and in relation to the factors he could control.)

This success gave him extra ideas. He divided the customers into three types: introverts unsure of themselves, extroverts very sure of themselves, and in-betweens, then he varied his presentation based on the customer's type. To the first he presented and talked more, to the latter, less and let them talk, and the ones in between he let talk, but when they paused, he talked. Very soon Jay was nudging 25% payout, but not quite there.

What was he missing?

INFO GATHERING IMPROVES RESULTS

Finally, he began to ask the customers more about themselves, trying to get to know what they really wanted the watch for. He divided the customers again into those who bought to impress (50% of them), those who needed it for work (30%), and others, who had special requirements (to know the time both in NY and in India, for example). Once he learned that, his entire presentation centered on the customer's needs, not the watch.

REACHING PEAK PERFORMANCE

That week he soared through 25%, and stayed there. On the Friday before the weekend, when commissions were paid, the boss came to Jay and said he already had a wife, but if he didn't, he'd propose to him. Jay smiled and said he'd consider it, if he were so naturally inclined, but he wasn't. Also, this would be his last month, since he was aiming to go back to school, to get an MBA. The boss was grief-stricken, and offered to raise jay's commission to 30%, if he kept it a secret, but Jay declined again, yet promised to stay in touch.

A month later Jay enrolled in the MBA program, and two years later graduated and joined the consulting company, where he met my family member who learned of his story. Soon Jay made a junior partner, but after two years as consultant (a most successful one, let me stress), he left and started a hedge fund.

SAME PRINCIPLE WORKS IN YOUR SLEUTHING, TOO

What specific tasks can you apply Jay's methods to, in your sleuthing?

Recruiting and interviewing informers should be among the first: there, too, you can track what works, which approach, what questions, especially Jay's last method of focusing on the other person at first, not the company or the product. What other factors could you try? How about the time of day, what you said, who talked first, what about? In sum, track what worked and what didn't. You will be surprised how fast you'll improve.

Then once you start tracking your investment actions (see last chapter), obvious topics of using Jay's (or rather Leela's) method will present themselves to you. In a way this is also what a champion sprinter does, when her coach videotapes each of her starts, paying attention to the angle of her ankle, the position of her toes, then tracking which works best for her, a millimeter here, a half-degree angle change there, and before she knows it, the champ has shaved a full half a second off her world record.

As an aside: when I ran the research at BBN, the top Canadian research boutique, all my five analysts became ranked #1 in their respective fields (me too), in a year and a half, essentially using the Jay/Leela method. Doing more of what works, and stopping doing what doesn't. Day by day, bit by bit. Again and again, and again.

A PROFOUND CHANGE OF MINDSET: NO LONGER A SCIENTIST

The above method is really a huge change of mindset: science is a collection of theories about how ontological reality works (as expressed in squiggles). So if you see yourself as a scientist (even unconsciously), you are occupied with attribution and causation: how this caused that, and why. But once you are a sleuth, or a chess-playing Neural Net (or Jay), you don't really care much about attribution. You only care *whether* some things worked, and then you do more of them; or whether they didn't, and then you don't. It's not for you to ask why. Just enjoy your success, and your money. And the time off.

Alright, then.

You now have half the story: how to keep improving your game of taking CFAs' money. But before getting to the story's *other* half, about the Dark Info hiding in your brain, we must close one more loophole. And that one has to do with the Hilbert problem we left for last. DH #6.

Yes, the one that asks if you can forecast the world's entire behavior *only* via ink squiggles.

CHAPTER 8
PHYSICISTS' POINT OF VIEW

Is the world discovered or created? Both. And the mysterious observer.

Now what about DH #6?

What *edge* can this bit of physicists' viewpoint give *you*, in your quest to take OPM?

To cut down on the suspense, let me give you the executive summary up front:

EXECUTIVE SUMMARY:

THE KEY IS THE OBSERVER—BOTH IN PHYSICS AND IN SLEUTHING.

In *classical* physics, not only does the data describe the world completely (i.e., reductionism is taken as given), but the entire data has also existed before anyone has even viewed it, no matter who did the measurement and who did the viewing.

So just go ahead and do science, *whoever you are*, and you'll know everything. Eventually. Hilbert says so. Einstein (before Quantum Physics), believed it too. Physicists' calls this belief "Realism."

Something like Tolstoy's history, where the leader doesn't matter and must obey reality's diktat.

And, the same belief is shared by classical/CFA investors: the financial data already exists in databases, audited, verified, certified, ready for *anyone* to manipulate, and it *describes the entire company*. No need for any *other* data. Just go ahead and pick stocks, whoever you are, and you'll outperform the market. Graham and Dodd say so. All CFAs believe in it.

And if you are an Internet-screen "investor," so must you.

On the other hand:

In modern, *quantum* physics, reductionism does *not* work, the world (like Dostoevsky's history), exists in a state of *many* possibilities, and information about it does *not* exist before a *specific* observer *categorizes* the data and *measures* it— *in the category of his or her choice*, as per Niels Bohr. So, in a sense, *the observer/measurer creates the information. And therefore, yes, it's only good for him or her.*

SLEUTH INVESTING, LIKE QUANTUM PHYSICS, GOOD FOR THE OBSERVER ONLY

The 2022 Physics Nobel Prize winners proved (yet again) that this last view is correct. Which is directly analogous to modern investing, i.e., sleuthing. Here, too, *the corporation exists in a state of many possibilities*, and much of its *info does not even exist* before you, the sleuth, query it, in the category of *your* choice. Thus, modern (i.e., sleuth) investing does *not* see the investor as a mere *consumer* of *passive* info. Rather, **every sleuth investor creates his or her own exclusive info**—which had not existed before he/she had dug for it.

And—this is key— this newly created info is exclusive to *this* sleuth only, because he/she had *chosen the category* to sleuth at. Each sleuth has to make this choice. As you must.

The obvious question is:

Why would you choose *this* particular category, in *this* particular case? For example, why choose to sleuth the true real estate value? Why not the CEO's true character? Or employees' opinions of the corporate plans? In simple words, *how do you make the choice of which category* of the company merits your attention and time *at this point*?

And the answer:

This choice is based on *your* experience, *your* preparation, and *your* gut instinct. All of them "System 1" related, which CFA investors do *not* use. They only use "System 2," by the book.

Some of these "System 1" abilities may be innate in you, but if not, they can be developed by having to use them on the fly, as you query more informers and get more gut feel for what's true and what isn't, what to ask next, or perhaps just when to keep quiet and let them talk. Like what we saw in nearly all the case studies. All were done using "System 1" thinking, by doing physical sleuthing, instinctively.

Just like General Vernon Walters did when he queried his East German informers, or like Nikita Khrushchev did, when he bullied JFK to get a measure of his character, or like Putin did when he queried a visiting minister to gauge if he was an initiator or an acceptor, and like I did, when I queried IBM employees about their views of the CEO and the board.

In each of these cases, an *active* observer created the information, along a category chosen by instinct and experience. *Information that others did not have.*

How to get better at this craft? How to see what works and what doesn't work—for *you*? And, finally and at last, how to access the uncategorized Dark Info hidden in your brain? The one that can give you the real edge?

This will be shown in the next two chapters, but I hope you already got a sense of it, by reading about Jay's methods.

NOW AN IMPORTANT NOTICE:

The rest of this chapter is for the physicists (and physics enthusiasts) among you—it's further proof of the statements about DH#6. The non-physicists can skip it and go straight to the final comparative analogy at the end of this chapter.

Still here? Don't say I didn't warn you…

Ok. Let's go on, then.

WHY HILBERT QUESTION #6 IS KEY

In his sixth question, Hilbert asked whether it's possible to develop physics from first principles, that is: axiomatize physics, as the Greeks have done to geometry, and as he suggested (in his DH#2 question) to be done to math.

In other words, *DH#6 asks whether physics can be developed entirely using math symbols,* i.e., whether the world can be entirely described via categories denoted in squiggles.

Yes, reductionism again.

Our interest is of course in the *commercial* world, but the answer to DH#6 would include it: Can you capture *all* info about physical stuff, i.e., assets, via numbers and symbols?

HILBERT'S SIXTH QUESTION'S TWO PARTS

Hilbert's question really has two parts:

The first part has to do with the world of big things, in which we live and invest, i.e., the world of *classical* physics where big things interact like billiard balls, based on known rules. Or, as physicists call it, **the IR world** (or infrared). Here, mathematics work.

The analogous equivalent in the commercial world would be the interaction between different companies, via accounting's debits and credits, assets and liabilities, revenues and costs, profit and loss. On that level, the math of commerce—accounting—works splendidly.

But **the second** part of DH#6 is **the UV world** (or ultraviolet). That's the world of micro-distances inside the atom, or the so-called Planck-scale, and here math doesn't always work. That's where quantum physics' Schrödinger equation works, but cannot be understood. In other words, the human brain cannot create inside itself a neuronal structure that mimics the structure of the subatomic world, because the human brain (or rather the cortex) is by evolution a *categorizing* machine, while the UV world isn't.

THE COMMERCIAL UV WORLD—RELATIONS INSIDE COMPANIES

The analogous equivalent in investing would be the company's *internal* relationships, and those between the "human particles," which can no longer be described in math—indeed often cannot completely be described in symbols, or "language" of any kind. For example, the fuzzy relationship between Steve Jobs and Pepsi's Sam. Or the low opinion of IBM's top management held by the rank and file. So, again, this is where the info advantage tilts to the sleuth.

Back now to Hilbert:

In his #6 question, he asked whether physics can be axiomatized not just for the macro world, but also for what he called the "quanta" world, what today physicists called the UV world.

Can it be done?

Because if it can be, then perhaps (by analogy) CFAs can somehow use accounting data to find out (in future) more about companies and people *internally*, and so reduce sleuths' info edge?

Fortunately, the answer is a no (or at most a low-likelihood maybe) for the first part of DH#6, but a definite no for the second part of it.

DH#6 FIRST PART WAS PROVEN, SORT OF

Yes, the first part of DH#6 (about the macro world) was arguably proven in the 1930s by Andrey Kolmogorov (yes, the one whom we've met before), who developed the science of probabilities from first principles.

Does this mean, then, that we *can* describe macro physics entirely by using ink squiggles, i.e., that reductionism in physics *does* work? Because if it does, it might mean there may be a way of forcing accounting to tell us more about the company than it is telling now, and then we *could* (maybe, one day) stay home and go click-click buy-sell based on accounting only.

So, can we?

No, we can't. First, because the ink squiggles that Kolmogorov used—aka math of probabilities—describe not *actual* physical events, but only *chances* of their occurrences. That is, his proof uses *a math of fictions* describing *other* fictions. Not good enough.

So what of the second part of DH#6?

Can the micro/quanta world be axiomatized too, even halfway, i.e., developed via math? That UV world of course is not used in commerce (unless it's in some high-tech microchip businesses), but perhaps its *analogy* would let us get more info about people, maybe?

DH#6 SECOND PART NOT SOLVED YET

It's generally accepted that it hasn't, i.e., Hilbert's sixth problem's second part (and as a result DH#6 in total) remains open. And in a future solution, as Wiki drily puts it, "the semantics of physics is expected to play a central role."

Ah yes, semantics, as in language. That is, ink squiggles describing physics on the smaller scale. Yes, yes, reductionism yet again.

But it gets worse for physicists.

DH#6'S SECOND PART VERY LIKELY SOLVED, AND THE ANSWER IS NO

Because the answer to DH#6's second part is not just "indeterminate," but *very probably a firm No.* That is, *in some parts of physics (the micro, UV world) there are* no *categories*, no variables, and so no math. In other words, some parts of the physical world cannot be probed using math, which needs variables, which in turn need categories.

But, without getting into the reasons, how *sure* can we be of this?

Extremely sure—at the 13-sigma level, if you care to know. And if that's really so (it is, proven), then (by analogy), sleuths who stay at physical-facts level can truly get internal corporate information *not* available to CFAs, who only stay at the ink-and-bits level. Because the full *physical* info spectrum of assets—like info about people—can *not* be wholly containable in math and words. Some of it (like real current value of real estate) will *always* remain at the physical level, **waiting for an observer to categorize it**, then take this info and use it privately.

But wait, you say. I (that is you, the reader), *am* a physicist, so you can tell me how it was proven. Go ahead!

Alright, then. You didn't skip this chapter, and asked for it. So here is the proof.

It all started with the paradox that even Einstein (and two collaborators) could not fix.

EPR, OR THE END OF LOCALITY

A key tenet in Einstein's theory of relativity is that nothing can go faster than the speed of light in a vacuum. However, if this is indeed so, how to explain the following?

Assume a particle just split into two sub-particles. Sub-particle A flies right, sub-particle B flies left. Because, pre-split, the parent-particle had zero spin (which is an attribute of some particles), then for the departing sub-particles we can say that (1) once we learn that A has a negative spin, then (2) we know *immediately* that B has a positive spin, for a total sum of zero.

So where is the paradox?

Ah. It is in the timing of "*once* we learn about A" and "*then* we know abut B," i.e., we know *immediately*.

But know how, immediately?

This, according to Einstein, should be impossible.

In quantum physics, you cannot know what a split-particle's spin is, until you *measure* it. The spin can then be either positive or negative, with 50% chance for each. (Yes, Kolmogorov's probability.) But assume that you've just measured the spin of sub-particle A, and it came out as positive.

What, then, about sub-particle B?

Sub-particle B is already parsecs away. Yet *at the very instant* you've learned about A's spin, you *instantly knew* with *100% certainty* (no more Kolmogorov here) that B has a negative spin. And there's no evading the point that *you knew this instantly, no matter how far away particle B was.*

The question is:

How did this info *get* to you? Because, since sub-particle B is now v-e-e-e-ry far away, it appears *the info about B's spin got to you from there to here faster than the speed of light.*

How come?

After all, Einstein postulated that nothing can go faster than light in vacuum. So, is Einstein's theory of relativity wrong? It cannot be, because everything *else* it forecasts perfectly. (Via math squiggles, yes.)

SPOOKY ACTION AT A DISTANCE

And yet, the above clearly demonstrates "spooky action at a distance," in Einstein's words.

A paradox. Which is another word for "it can't be, and yet it is."

This seeming paradox (known as EPR) created a big problem for Einstein's theory, so he and two collaborators (Podolsky and Rosen) came up with a fixit-idea. There must be (they said) *hidden variables inside particles*, a sort of subatomic DNA, internal to *all* particles, that dictate their *future* behavior too, even *after* splitting, no matter where they were.

Sounds rickety?

It sure does. It's like assuming there are hidden accounting categories in between the lines of the financial statements that would tell us more about the company than CFAs can now know—for example, about the CEO's character— if only we knew how to look for them, via accounting methods that have not *yet* been invented—but one day will be.

Hidden debits and credits, if you will.

Make sense?

Of course not. And it's the same for the "hidden variables" theory in physics. So why did Einstein and his two collaborators need them, and why did they stick with them for a while?

They did it just so that they (and other physicists) could say that the *equation forecasting particles' behavior*—physics' equivalent of accounting—was *still* valid. That is, that the system of ink squiggles/categories (or "formalism," in Einstein's words) was still reliable *everywhere*, big or small. IR or UV. Only we are not *yet* smart enough to find these extra variables.

Yet.

But in future we will. That is, the EPR's debate is also about the "yet."

Sound familiar?

Sure does. Remember the 1900 math congress in Paris? And the debate about reductionism?

Bois-Reymond said, no, some things we *never* will know, because some things we *can't* know. Hilbert said yes we will, one day, because we must, and because it would be terrible if we can't. Besides, if we can't, then math (and physics, too) would have a big hole in the middle, which we'll never be able to convert to squiggles on which to do "System 2" thinking (aka science.) And because we (both mathematicians and physicists) use *only* math to do science, this would be just terrible.

The same of course can be said about investing. It would just be terrible (to CFAs) if it is proven (as this book tries to do) that the financial statements, and numbers, cannot contain *all* information about companies and stocks.

So who was right? Hilbert or Bois-Reymond?

If Bois-Reymond was right, then (by analogy) sleuths have a big advantage, because the physical facts that sleuths unearth, CFAs can never know. But if Hilbert was right, somehow, then CFAs— one day—could stay home and go click-click, if only they learned how to go about it the right way—and take sleuths' money.

In simple words:

Okay, CFAs can't do it *yet*, but maybe one day they will. And then, one day CFAs might learn *almost* everything that sleuths can. (The "almost" is about people, because the Turing Test, like Shakespeare, still says that people are un-categorizable.)

So which is it? And where is the proof I promised all you physicists?

THERE AIN'T NO HIDDEN VARIABLES

For a long while, EPR's view held, because physicists did not like to admit limitations to their work, just as the "*Ignoramus* yes, *Ignorabimus* no" view of Hilbert held, until Gödel.

EPR's view held until 1964, when an impish Irish physicist, John Stewart Bell, proposed an experiment that involved counting probabilities (à la Kolmogorov), which would *prove* that in the EPR paradox, *there cannot be, indeed there aren't any, hidden variables.*

In other words, *at the micro-level, the UV world, there are no hidden categories.* None. Zip. Which either meant that there *was* instantaneous communication between the A and B sub-particles, and then Einstein was wrong—or that *categories did not exist in the UV world.* That is, the two sub-particles may *look* like two different things, but in fact *they were still one*, so what happens to one also happens to the other, lickety-split.

Or, in physics terminology, there was no "locality."

Which, by the way, is a kissing cousin of the so-called Pauli Exclusion Principle to the physicists among you.

And, for you brave non-physicist readers:

NO LOCALITY—SO EVERYTHING IS DIFFERENT, OR MAYBE IS THE SAME?

Wolfgang Pauli was a physicist of genius who found many splendid things about the quantum universe. One principle of his is called the Pauli Exclusion Principle (PEP), which says that no two particles can have the same quantum numbers. In rough approximation, it means that no two particles can occupy the same quantum seat.

The problem is (yes, it's another paradox): at every moment, new particles are popping into existence and others popping out. So (here is the paradox): How can a newly popped-in particle know all the q-particulars of all q-seats of *every* other particle *everywhere*? So that it wouldn't go to sit (by mistake) in an already-occupied q-seat? Not just of *one* far-away particle, as in EPR, but of *any and all* particles in the universe? Most v-e-e-ery far away? Yet this newborn particle does seem to know all this, because the PEP is valid. So how come? And doesn't it constitute a massive spooky action (or rather knowledge, leading to action) at a distance? Like the A and B sub-particles from the EPR paradox, only writ v-e-e-ery large?

Or maybe, just maybe, like the A and B sub-particles of EPR, in one respect the *entire* universe is a single huge, happy category? A huge "thing-in-itself," a Kantian *ding-am-sich*, its own sui-generis, a giant Kolmogorov-random string? Containing its own hidden variables everywhere? (Yes, there is such a theory.)

I won't go into the implications (because this, after all, is neither a book of physics nor of philosophy), but go straight to the obvious question of why should we care, i.e., what are the implications, or at least the analogies, to sleuth investing?

It is obviously this: if particles are analogous to people, and their interactions analogous to the interactions among people, both outside and inside companies, then we can make a direct (though a mite poetic) comparison. Just as new particles are born every moment, each and every one of them miraculously different, so are new people born every moment, each and every one of them—of us—different, just like micro particles or minuscule snowflakes.

ALL HUMANS ARE DIFFERENT

So yet again: How come? Because, you know, we are. Different, that is. Each and every one of us is unique. We all have different and unique DNA. So unique, that its uniqueness is accepted as physical evidence—physical, not fictional and circumstantial—in every court, not just Judge Turing's.

So here is the coda that the last aria has been leading to: How then can all this splendiferous human richness of differences and abilities and flaws and uncategorizables be born anew every moment, each one of us unknowingly different?

And the sleuthing twinned-question:

How can the above so blithely be ignored in that ultimate fictional creation, the commercial corporation, which is at the base of all modern human civilization? Which today is described by CFAs only via the thin gruel of Pacioli's Summa?

BUT SOME PARTICLES ARE THE SAME

After all, unlike some identical *categorized* particles—an electron is an electron is an electron, and a positron is a positron is a positron—every non-categorizable human is splendidly different than all other humans. You and me and Steve Jobs and Lee Iacocca and the CEO of Small Conglomerate and the head server at Fancy Eats (who could see the rascal's character at a glance) and the honest machinist on Dana's shop floor, we are all different and unique, each one of us.

And yet, CFAs and others of their ilk totally ignore this. How can they? And if you don't, how can you avoid taking their money?

Now back to the A and B sub-particles, because we still haven't established whether there really are no hidden variables (i.e., categories, i.e., math) in the seam between classical physics of the IR, and quantum physics of the UV.

WAS BELL RIGHT? YES HE WAS: EXCEEDINGLY LIKELY

So is this true? Was John Stewart Bell right?

Unfortunately for Einstein and Podolsky and Rosen: it is, and he was.

Several experiments were done since, with pairs of photons, one proving Bell's conjecture true at the 6-sigma level (e.g., by Proietti and his team), another (by Giustina and her team) at the 13-sigma level. (Just look them up on ArXiv.org. If you are physicist, you'd know it.)

Which is as close to a certainty as any (practical) scientist could wish for. (And in fact, just before this book went to print, Alain Aspect, John Clauser and Anton Zeilinger won the 2022 Nobel Prize in Physics for their experiments proving the above *beyond* doubt.)

OCCAM'S RAZOR

Seven hundred years ago, Sir William of Occam proposed that if you have two theories that equally fit the facts, choose the simpler one. In this case, the two theories are: (1) There are no *hidden* variables in the UV world, and (2) There are no variables there *at all.*

The second one is simpler. So, since Einstein's theory does work, the best answer is that indeed, in the UV world, or rather in the seam between it and the IR world, there are no categories at all, and therefore no math.

So: *in some parts of the physical world, there are no categories, no math, and so no measurements.* Therefore, our cortex, which is what **invents** categories (like math, or chess EFs, or Pacioli's accounting), doesn't work there either.

And by analogy, there are parts of the *commercial* world too (like people, or their intra-company relations, and also some aspects of physical assets), where accounting stops working.

What *is* working there, then?

NO REDUCTIONISM IN MATH, PHYSICS, PEOPLE—OR ACCOUNTING

For this we have to return to quantum physics' concept of the observer (which you met in the Executive Summary), and see how he/she/it is applicable to investing also. And once you see that, the entire theory of sleuth investing should fall into place for you. Then you can go ahead and practice it by sleuthing, and by looking for the Dark Info, the kind hidden someplace inside your brain, and use it to take CFAs' money—and, what's more, keep getting better and better at it, a la Leela, and Jay, and Lee Kuan Yew.

It all hinges on the observer.

THE MYSTERIOUS OBSERVER

This observer stands like a ghost in the midst of modern physics—just like the Investor does in the midst of classical CFA investing.

In classical physics—or classical investing—it wouldn't matter *who* the observer/investor was. Because in both cases *the observer is deemed to* be a *classical scientist*, so what he/she/it does, whether physics or investing, is settled (classical) science; and *in classical science the scientist doesn't matter*. All results would be the same no matter who *does* the experiment, or who *reports* it. Einstein or Michelson. Bohr or Pauli. Newton or Fermi.

Or so, at least, was the case in classical physics before the newfangled quantum physics came along—and so was the case in classic CFA investing before the newfangled sleuth investing arrived, both saying that *some info can have no squiggles to describe it*, none, and so must always stay physical—and *personal*.

MECHANIZING CLASSICAL PHYSICS AND CLASSICAL INVESTING

And all the while, because both classical physics and classical investing subscribed (implicitly) to reductionism (all info is in data, and it tells anyone and everyone everything), classical physics and classical investing tried to mechanise/automate their processes.

Physics did this by providing mechanical math formulas whose input is always the same, no matter who uses the formula, no matter who measured the data, no matter who reported the results. And CFA investing did this by mechanizing stock picking into a science of Evaluation Functions, no matter who uses them, no matter which auditor provided the financial statements, no matter which investor (or Algo) came to the Buy or Sell decision.

In all this, both classical physics and classical investing dispensed with the individual scientist and the individual investor—the formula's/method's user. The numbers were the numbers, the process was the process, and the user was fungible. Non-numerical data did not matter. Indeed, it had no meaning.

THE FUNGIBLE INVESTOR

Ben Graham pitched buying stocks below WC/share, or better still, below Net-Net/share. And if one did that, then one could ignore the company's business, its management, its products, customers, even the legal regime under which the company operated (Xi Jinping's and Putin's too) and so didn't care how strong or weak was your ownership, because that last was non-categorizable.

Everything was in the financial numbers which one manipulated. And of course, this "one" investor could also be anyone, even you, so long as you did it by the numbers. Because investing was practically a science.

Click-click, buy-sell, have another coffee.

Or was it?

THE GHOST IN THE (REDUCTIONIST) MACHINE

Perhaps it is not surprising that value investing thought itself a science, needing only numerical input, irrespective of the inputter or the valuer or the measurer, because *the very basis of value investing was Pacioli's accounting*, and that science, too, dispensed with anything beyond the numbers. The company's business didn't matter, the CEO didn't matter, management didn't matter, the legal regime didn't matter. Only the financial numbers did. They contained all information.

Or did they?

For CFAs, they sure did. Just as in classical physics only the numbers did. And there, too, they were provided a priori, no matter by whom, and could be used by anyone, and they contained everything anyone needed.

Same as in physics, until EPR's adherents realized (to their shock) that the numbers and formulas apparently *didn't* contain everything. Neither did value investors bother with the inputter or the investor or the auditor (who could be Arthur Andersen too). Neither CP nor CI bothered about the observer. However, that mysterious ghost really mattered both in physics and investing. Hence the silent shock when, for the last 15 years, value investing stopped working.

BLIND ACCEPTANCE OF REDUCTIONISM THE ROOT PROBLEM

In both these disciplines, physics and investing, the blind acceptance of reductionism meant that the world—whether the physical universe or the commercial one—could be entirely described via its categories, and that these *existed separately and independently of the observer.*

Then came the new quantum physicists, who advanced the idea that the *observer*—the one who took the measurement—mattered too, and mattered a great deal. Indeed, the observer was at the very heart of modern physics. Or, as Niels Bohr (one of the fathers of quantum physics) put it: *all measurement starts with an act of will*—i.e., deciding *which* category to measure.

Just like now it seems that the individual sleuth investor/observer, is at the heart of investing.

But let's get it straight here:

FOR EINSTEIN, OBSERVERS WERE MANY, YET ALL WERE VALID

Oddly enough, Einstein actually said that the observer did *not* matter. But he said it as a sequel to his first quadruple postulates of the theory of relativity: (1) The speed of light in vacuum is finite, (2) That speed is always the same, (3) Nothing goes faster than that, and 4. *All observers' viewpoints are equally valid.*

That fourth point was a bit strange, because it also implied that *several observers' viewpoints could be different*—i.e., that different observers could come up with different measurements. And yet all were valid.

The above of course would be shocking to classical physicists, for whom the observer was fungible. (Something like CEOs or CFOs are to a CFA, or leaders to Tolstoyan historians.) But equally shocking was Einstein's emphatic statement that *all* these observers' viewpoints, whether the same or not, were equally *valid.*

But valid how, if different? And from *whose* point of view? Yet *another* observer? Who? God? The "old one" whom Einstein said doesn't play dice?

Now here you are probably getting impatient, and are asking insistently: Why the heck do I need all this stuff about physics in a book about sleuth investing?

Because the similarity between the two is striking, which leads us to the ultimate payoff:

IN INVESTING, TOO, OBSERVERS/SLEUTHS ARE MANY AND ALL THEIR VIEWPOINTS ARE EQUALLY VALID

A basic tenet of sleuthing is that, besides financial information, provided by outside paid observers/auditors and known to all, *there are also infinitely varied, privately obtained (or created) physical information* that a sleuth investor, acting as an *active observer*—that is, a *participant*—can create for his or her own use.

Which brings up odd parallels, because this is close to Marx's view, who said that the role of the philosopher is not to *observe* history (i.e., act like a classical, passive physicist), but rather to help *change and create* it.

Yes, just like a Dostoevskyan historian, or like a modern quantum physics' observer—or yes, like a modern sleuth investor who creates his or her *own* info.

Yes, *creates.* Not discovers, or observes, but *creates.*

And believe it or not, no matter how varied are these infinities of privately sleuthed info, as numerous as the number of sleuths, and as different as each sleuth's different approaches, they are *all* equally valid (like Einstein's observers), and *all should lead to market overperformance.* Although not always by the same degree, since that depends on the individual sleuth's skill, ingenuity, and experience, and—perhaps mainly—*choice of category* in which he or she determines to sleuth that particular stock.

But determine how?

That of course (yes) depends on his or her skill, ingenuity and experience.

COMMERCIAL REALITY, LIKE PHYSICAL REALITY, IS BOTH DISCOVERED AND CREATED

Which, by the way, also parallels quantum physics' main question (which, in turn, oddly parallels that of history's prime question): Is reality discovered, or created?

The answer is of course, both.

Reality, as per the parable of Plato's Cave, is what goes on *outside* the cave. Or, as philosophers call it, ontological reality. But that reality is of course unknown to us cave-dwellers. What we human observers/prisoners-in-our-body "know" is only what we experience of it, via reality's *categorized* versions. This is after our sensory inputs have gone through our cortex which, having discarded the non-categorizable portion—the Dark Info—has turned the sensory mish-mash into words and numbers and formulas and charts.

Like physics' formulas, or math's symbols, or accounting's debits and credits, yes. All are mere categorized squiggles of the real, ontological stuff.

And in that sense, if you are doing CFA analysis, your investing brain creates a *categorized reality* for you in the form of accounting, in order to pick stocks. But then, like the sucker at the poker table, you become the designated loser for all us sleuths out there, who see also what you don't, what you can't, as this book is trying to teach you to see. Because sleuths, like good poker players, don't just look at the cards, but also at faces, and at human interaction, and they remember past games, like Leela, where certain facial expressions preceded a win or a loss on the part of the other player.

And sleuths do it how?

Not just via "System 2" thinking (although yes, they do remember cards), but also by instinct, i.e., "System 1."

As Hugo Duminil-Copin, math professor extraordinaire at the University of Geneva and a worldwide probability theory expert, said: *risk, or chance, doesn't really exist, because* chance, the real one, is **that which cannot be predicted, no matter what tools are used.**

So there it is: there are parts of the world—the commercial world too—which cannot be predicted using categories, and math, and formulas.

NO GRAND UNIFIED THEORY—IN BOTH PHYSICS AND STOCKS

Which also means that there can be no "Theory of Everything" (aka TOE) or a "Grand Unified Theory" (aka GUT) in physics, because, due to John Bell's (proven) finding, we know that some parts of physics *cannot* be expressed in squiggles, which is what a "theory" is made of.

Similarly in our case, we must accept that *there cannot be a comprehensive predictive formula for stock prices*, based only on the (squiggles in the) financial statements: a few key company factors will always stay physical, waiting for a sleuth investor to dig them out physically, à la Niels Bohr, keep them private, and so take the money of CFAs who base their investment decisions on public financial squiggles alone. (But see also Appendix 2, regarding Jim Simons' Renaissance Technologies.)

A TRIPLE COMPARATIVE ANALOGY

Now for both the physicists among you and those who skipped to the end of the chapter, let's see if we can **compare doing science to doing investing**, and (sure, why not) also **to chess playing by Neural Net computers**.

Let's add computerized chess and use the Turing Test as an overriding metaphor, to summarize the triple analogy:

ANALOGIES OF PHYSICS, CHESS, AND INVESTING, BOTH CLASSICAL AND NEW

- **Classical physics** views the world via the "Turing slot of math," just as CFA investors view the world of commerce via the "Turing slot of accounting."

- **Quantum physics** views world info as if created by the individual Observer, just as sleuth investors view stock info as if created by the individual sleuth.

- **First-generation chess-playing computers** view the chess board via the "Turing slot of EF math," while **second-generation chess-playing computers** view it via the "Turing slot of this individual Neural Net's past success and failure."

Or, separated into old and new:

Chess:
Old: First-generation computer chess queries the *chessboard* via the Turing Slot of EF.
New: A modern chess computer is an observer querying its *own* experience and memory.

Physics:
Old: Classical physics is querying the universe via the Turing Slot of mathematics.
New: Quantum physics is the observer querying the universe, judging future forecasting success by *his or her own experience of the universe's past responses to his or her queries.*

Investing:
Old: Classic CFA investing is querying business via the narrow Turing Slot of accounting
New: Sleuth investing is a sleuth's *individual experience* in querying a business for non-categorizable info, along his or her own choice of categories to sleuth, based on his / her past success.

LOADING YOUR BRAIN WITH SLEUTHED, PHYSICAL FACTS

Take a deep breath. It is almost over.

Are you convinced that sleuth investing is the way to go, if you want to outperform the market?

And if you are, would you like to know how you can do it?

Here is how:

- First, learn all the CFA squiggle-facts. Read all the filings. Know thy opponent.

- Second, load your brain with *physical* facts that you *yourself* have dug out, so as to push your brain into "System 1" thinking. (See my first book for the method.) Only this way will you get info that is invisible to CFAs (what I called the Dark Info) but that is visible to you—and you only —within the original, non-categorized total ply.

- Third, your brain can now at last access your Dark Info, practically on its own.

The next chapter should finally show you how.
(Hint: It's to do with emotion. Yours.)

CHAPTER 9

BRAIN SCIENTISTS' POINT OF VIEW

Lady Gaga, Tony Bennett's cortex, Neural Net, and—finally—Dark Info.

In the early 2010s, the singer-crooner Tony Bennett began to forget faces, names, and people he had known all his life. That's what happens sometimes when one grows old. So in 2014, at the behest of Tony's son and Lady Gaga (with whom Tony had sung before), Tony performed with Lady Gaga one more time. It was marketed (kind of) as his last performance.

Luckily, Tony could still recall many of his popular hits. Still, everyone realized that this show would probably be Tony's last, and so tickets sold out quickly. But it was a good thing to have had that show, because soon after it, Tony's mind seemed to slip deeper into forgetfulness, confusion, and often blankness. So much so that three years after that double show with Lady Gaga, in 2017, Tony's wife took him to his doctor, who diagnosed him as suffering from Alzheimer's disease. It was no longer just old age. It meant Tony was destined to lose his memory entirely and not be able to remember his friends, his family—and his music.

THE LONG SLIDE INTO THE MIND'S NIGHT

In medical terms, Tony's hippocampus had stopped doing its job. Just as the cortex's job is to categorize incoming data, then use the output to forecast, think, and plan actions, the hippocampus' job is to form, organize, and store memories of thinking and actions and actions' results. Then, it retrieves them when needed from wherever they'd been stored, whether in pre-fixed brain locations or a sort of distributed cloud.

Please note, though: as Leela does it, memories of your past actions' *results* are stored also, alongside passive memories of faces, names, and places. The past actions' results are used (upon retrieval) as an extra input for the cortex's ongoing forecasting. Because what past actions had led to—i.e., their success/failure—is an important criterion for the cortex's Neural Net's current decision of whether a contemplated action is wise, foolish, or anything in between.

Therefore, when the hippocampus' function starts failing, so does the cortex's ability to forecast, and so does its owner's ability to think, decide, and do.

This by the way is not just a conjecture. It was actually proven in recent research done at University College of London, where professor Eleanor Maguire found that people with damage to their hippocampus not only had difficulty remembering their past, but they also had difficulty thinking of future actions. Probably because forecasting the future requires correlations with past experience—"System 1" thinking, in other words, aka instinct.

Like Leela's chess playing, yes.

For example, for a singer—or a jazz player—it would be the question whether a contemplated vibrated note, in response to the accompanist's cue, would deliver the reaction it had always delivered before, to a similar audience. It's the "similar" and the "reaction" and the "before" which are the hippocampus's responsibility. The "contemplated" is the cortex's; the second cannot work without the first.

MIND AND MEMORY SLIDE INTO THE ABYSS

Now, however, as Tony aged and his Alzheimer's intensified, his hippocampus faded and memories faded with it. Tony's conversations faltered, he mumbled, and his interaction with friends and family turned awkward—often he didn't know who they were. And once Tony's condition became known—the family did not make a secret of it—his fans and admirers realized that they'd never hear Tony Bennett singing on stage again, whether alone or with others; that his 2014 concert with Lady Gaga was most likely his last.

But seven years after that 2014 dual-concert, in 2021, when Tony was already 94 years old, his son, who was also his manager, and Lady Gaga, suggested that she and Tony do one more concert, at Radio City Music Hall.

As Lady Gaga later told it, very few believed it could be pulled off, including she herself. She was therefore ready, she admitted, to have to perform much of the show herself if, once on stage, Tony could not do it.

FAINT HOPE, THEN BACK INTO THE TWILIGHT

There was some faint hope, though: in a rehearsal at his apartment overlooking New York, Tony's long-term accompanist later said that Tony seemed to remember more than others expected—it was as if the music brought memories back. But right after the rehearsal, Tony slipped back into the Alzheimer's twilight. The rehearsal's effect was fleeting.

Or could the music bring back some memories in the coming performance also? Everyone hoped it would, though it did not seem likely. Because when the day arrived, and Lady Gaga accompanied Tony from the limo to the hall, he shuffled after her amiably but again could not recognize her, calling her Sweetheart instead of by her name. Other people, too, he could not recognize. So without much hope Lady Gaga took him by the hand from the green room to the stage, and as the curtain rose, the hall, filled to the rafters with Tony's long-time admirers, erupted with claps and ovation, the surge of emotions almost palpable.

Lady Gaga curtsied to the public, blew Tony a kiss, and spread her hands before the audience. "Here is Tony Bennett!"

To her surprise and delight, the man who could not recognise her a few minutes before beamed and said, "*And here is Lady Gaga*!"

A MIRACLE TAKES PLACE

Everyone teared up, her too. And then she and Tony began to sing, one by one, then together—nearly nonstop. The singing lasted more than an hour, song after song, all the words, with ovations in between— "I Left My Heart In San Francisco", "Who Can I Turn To", "Fly Me To The Moon", and more, much more. Tony Bennett, whose Alzheimer's disease was so advanced that he could not recognize faces or names, not even the photo of Bob Hope, who years before had made him change his name from Anthony Dominick Benedetto to Tony Bennett, that man on stage now sang all his old songs, without notes, with hardly any errors. It all came back. All of it. The tunes, the words, the gestures, the twists in the voice, the emotion, the amazing musicality, the fabulous talent. Everything came back. It was as if Tony was 25 years younger, with all his memories, all his gestures, all his art intact. It all came back.

But how? And back from where?

CBS did a show about it, with Anderson Cooper narrating discreetly, letting the facts speak for themselves, allowing the people involved to present it in their own words. You cannot watch it all through without tearing up. My eyes moisten just remembering it. I hope yours do too.

But let's all of us wipe our eyes and ask ourselves: Where did these memories come from? From where?

Please remember: Tony's cortex was by now like a 94-year-old Swiss cheese, practically unfit for human use. His 94-year-old hippocampus was shot too, and thus the cortex's access to Tony's old memories, or whatever shadows were left of them, was gone also. Yet here they all were, those memories, back somehow, all of them: names, songs, gestures, the artistic trills, the emotions, both words and melodies, face and name recognition… It all came back.

DOES THE BRAIN DO BACKUPS?

But back from *where*?

Where has all this treasure been stored? And if so, when? And how often? And how does the brain retrieve these long-gone backups, as Tony's did in 2021, without even thinking about it? Can others do it too? And if so, what else can be retrieved?

CAN BRAIN-BACKUP RETRIEVAL BE TAUGHT, LEARNED?

And not just the words and the music came back, but also the emotions and the artistry. Not just the "System 2" thinking, recognizing faces and making conversation and deciding how to respond, then actually responding, but the entire "System 1" stuff too. That is, the instincts, the automatic decisions on-the-fly of a performer, and a master performer at that, the unique humanity, whatever that is, the kind that both Turing and Shakespeare said cannot be plumbed by words or numbers.

Where did this all come from?

If Tony's hippocampus, which both stores and directs memory storage and performs memory retrieval, was no longer working, then what *was*? And doing *what*?

The three obvious questions before us are these:

1. Where were the lost memories double-stored?
2. What drew these backups out?
3. And third, how?

And once we are at it, perhaps a fourth question, this time yours—the usual one:

4. How is all this relevant to your task of outperforming the market by taking CFAs' money?

WAS IT JUST THE MUSIC?

Tony's neurologist had an answer. She said it was partly "muscle memory" (whatever that is), because Tony's brain had practically hard-wired itself around the music. Music was at the base of Tony's brain's wiring, she said.

Or, in translation: Tony could recall the backup memories, because he was a master musician.

Does it mean, then, that others who are *not* musicians could *not* do it? And if it's only because of the music, why don't *other* Alzheimer's-stricken musicians report similarly miraculous memory recovery like Tony's?

Besides, why hadn't it happened to Tony before?

Come to think of it, it probably had, in that rehearsal in Tony's apartment in New York City, as reported by his accompanist. It wasn't as pronounced as in the performance, but still, it was there.

So maybe it *was* the music after all? But if so, why not as strongly as in the performance? What was it in the performance that brought it all back?

IT WAS MOST LIKELY THE EMOTION

One obvious conjecture is that the memories came back due to the strong *emotion* Tony felt once on stage, swept by the hot love his fans and the public were sending his way. That's what brought it all back, the hot emotion.

And yes, the neurologist did catch that part. "We all remember emotional memories far more than we do other types of memories," she said. **"Memories that are imbued with emotion—they're kind of pickled in it, as it were."**

So, is that how you, too, can access your non-categorized/discarded memories? By pickling them in emotion first? Can you do it consciously, or does it just happen?

And, once you *un*pickle the memories, can you *keep* them unpickled?

Sadly, Tony could not.

THE MAGIC RETRIEVAL DID NOT LAST

His magical memory retrieval lasted only to the end of the show. Whatever part of his brain his duplicated, backed-up memories were stored in, and which opened up for the show when triggered by the fans' love and Tony's own emotion, that brain part closed up again as the show ended. The magic was over.

But the question remains, though: What was the brain part that opened, then closed again?

This was the part that allowed Tony to make on-the-fly, *instinctive* decisions once again, based on memories accessible only by emotion, because *those memories had emotion as part of their long ago, not-yet-categorized "ply."* The personal emotions Tony felt when he had sung these songs before, the same feelings he felt now on stage.

EMOTION AS THE MAGIC KEY?

These emotions seem to be the key that opened the magic backup box. In other words, there is hidden info in your brain—and in your opponents' brain, too, the CFAs'—which is accessible not by a word or a number or any other symbol category, that is, "System 2" thinking—but by a feeling, an instinct, yet only the one *that has been created by you, when you yourself had stored the memory there, personally.*

A SHORT STROLL INTO YOUR BRAIN

The above deserves a side excursion into the brain—just a short stroll.

The limbic system, also known as the paleomammalian cortex, bestrides both sides of the thalamus, just below the cerebrum's medial temporal lobe in the forebrain. It *coordinates emotion, long-term memory, and sense of smell*, and so controls much of your emotional life and helps you generate long-term memories—which, please note, are attached to emotions. (Which is why Proust starts his magnum opus about lost time with a madeleine, the fragrant almond cookie.) The limbic system also processes lower-level sensory input, as well as the emotional reactions to them. Yes, emotions again. *This means that both long-term memories and the raw uncategorized senses, including gut sense, are attached to emotions,* which is not the case in categories—these come from the cortex and are processed dispassionately, via "System 2" thinking, as *names*. Per contra, the limbic system regulates emotional, visceral autonomic processes, i.e., instincts. Yes, it does have a sort of specialized cortex of its own, called the **entorhinal cortex**, but it is considered part of the limbic system. It deals mainly with memory and associations attached to it.

And what does all this mean for your investing?

INFO ATTACHED TO EMOTION IS A SLEUTH'S ADVANTAGE

It means that CFAs' use of "System 2" thinking is *dispassionate*, whereas sleuths, who certainly use "System 2" thinking too, also use "System 1," which is keyed by *emotions*.

Please note: not emotional *intelligence*, which is "System 2", but emotional *information*, "System 1."

INSTINCTIVE "SYSTEM 1" DECISIONS BEST AFTER SLEEPING ON THEM

Another key finding is that the *processing of new information into long-term memories takes place mainly during sleep*. So after you've sleuthed physical information and loaded your brain with raw facts, don't jump to conclusions straight away. Better sleep on it first, if you want to increase the reliability of your instinct (as per "System 1"). Otherwise, you may risk premature conclusions based on as-yet-undigested "named" information, straight from your CFA-type cortex.

But there also are other parts of the brain which participate in your sleuthing.

Besides memory filing, **memory retrieval is a joint effort by the limbic system's amygdala, hippocampus, and prefrontal cortex.** However, the neurons here are not like the neuronal columns in the cortex. Because the limbic system's function is to handle emotions too, a possible conjecture is that these neurons do not perform the same modeling as the regular cortex does (via the Vernon Mountcastle algo), but rather they **compare raw emotional and sensory input to past snapshots of similar constellations**—similar to what chess-playing Leela's Neural Network does. Here there are no decisions by categories as done by the main cortex, no names, just overall fit of raw physical inputs to past memories, full ply, seeking best fit with another total image. This is often keyed by emotions—or even smell, the sense most closely attached to emotions.

But just *where* is all this done? If both cortex and hippocampus are mostly shot, as Tony's were?

This is not entirely clear. It may be localized, or even distributed over several areas of the brain. But wherever this unnameable, full-ply info is located, whether a fixed spot or in several on-the-fly places, this is the part or parts of the brain whose long-term backup (probably) enabled Tony Bennett to recognize Lady Gaga even after his defunct cortex had lost all memory of her. *So that's most likely the part of your brain you want active in sleuthing.* But **to activate it, you have to charge it first** with physical details tied to emotion, then sleep on it. And to bring it up you have to recall the emotion you felt when you created the memory—e.g., when you talked to your informers, recalled the emotions they displayed, and the one you felt when they revealed their true opinions of their CEO, or when something in their voice broke through and you recognized the truth in it.

LIMBIC SYSTEM RESPONSIBLE FOR MOTIVATION TOO

And, this, too: a side benefit of storage in the limbic system is that **"System 1" is also responsible for motivation**. So when you activate the limbic system periodically while sleuthing, you'll also be activating your motivation, and so should find it much easier to turn off your Internet and go out and talk to people you've never talked to before. Your emotions will be up and humming, your mood will be up, and soon you'll be off your chair and out and about to learn **physical** facts CFAs have not even thought of. And learn them personally.

These kinds of personal facts will then be stored not just as words and numbers in your brain, but as life *events*, your life, just as an entire ply is memorized by Alpha Zero and Leela, not broken up into categories of Working Capital or Inventory on which to compute an EF, but retained as an entire ply, wrapped by your emotion that indicates its importance to *you*. And that emotion is what would give you the confidence to stick with a position, even when all others are selling. Because you'll know what CFAs don't. And that's because you've seen it, and heard it, and touched it, and smelled it. So your brain will retain it, and retain it whole.

Tony's brain, apparently—like all our brains—must have retained it whole, perhaps as a backup, because it was a different kind of retention, perhaps one that always goes on, but *is retrievable only in emotional emergencies.*

Just like the human body, which in these modern times feeds mostly on cheap sugar and other carbs and growing obese on them, is unable to unlock the energy stored in its fat, unless feeling acute starvation. On the other hand, athletes on a keto diet always have access to their fat—just like our carnivore forefathers had.

"SYSTEM 1", THE HEALTHIER BRAIN DIET

In a similar way, perhaps, CFAs, who are fattened on ready-made System-2 Value Line financials, are unable to unlock the hidden info available to sleuths who, like our more alert and physical ancestors, operate by "System 1" instinct, if fed on meat-and-fat *physical* data.

But wait, you say: How can we be sure of all this? What's the exact mechanism of info storage and retrieval, of such a brain backup, which helped Tony sing?

In a keto diet we do know the exact mechanism. (Look up the Physiology of Medicine Nobel Prize of 2016.) But here we don't. And if we don't know the mechanism, how can we be sure emotion is the cause and the key to the Dark Info? The kind that cannot be categorized and named? The kind Leela and Alpha Zero are using?

The answer is, we cannot know.

But please remember: *in the domain of "System 1" thinking, we don't care about attribution or causality.* Just like Leela and Alpha Zero, and Jay. We only care about *correlation*, that is: whether it was a highly likely co-factor in ultimate success, or not.

And, just like Leela learning how to win, or Jay learning how to sell better, *we don't care a whit why this action worked and that another didn't.* If it worked, Jay just did more of it. If it didn't, he dropped it. That's also how Lee Kuan Yew built Singapore. Ply by ply.

Somehow, in Tony's brain were etched the entire plies of his past performances, for each song.

As to why *these* were retained while loving family dinners and smiling friends' faces, were not retained? We don't know, but we can guess. Perhaps the emotions there were not as strong, or perhaps the deep *personal* involvement was not so deep.

EMOTIONS IMPORTANT BOTH TO YOU AND TO OTHERS, WHEN CREATED AND WHEN RETRIEVED

Perhaps what's key here is not just the emotion, but its importance. The importance to *you.* And the fact that it is deeply meaningful. Not just to you, but to others too, at the moment it's created—by you and those others.

General Vernon Walters' interaction with his informers was intense and personal, and so was his interaction with Gorby and Raisa. All knew that what was coming would be momentous. They were sure, and so were afraid, and told the truth.

Truth, in my experience, is easier to identify than lies. Many people lie, some very skillfully. I often stop trying to discover who and where and how. On the other hand, the truth has an aura all its own, a timbre of the voice, a tingle at the back of your neck. It's like reading great literature, or listening to great music, or seeing great art. You know it when you hear it, or see it, or feel it.

General Walters had, and he knew.

Per contra, Barkley's interactions with CIA back-office boffins and Foggy Bottom underlings who informed him of the formal collective's opinion, were neither intense, nor personal, nor meaningful. They were so far removed from the moment the info was obtained, that the only way to ascertain if the info was correct or not was by pure "System 2" bureaucratic logic, cold calculations, and perhaps a regression analysis by an enterprising math boffin.

Nothing to do with instinct or gut feel. Nothing personal.

Unlike General Walters' info, which was all of the above at once, and thus armor-coated with an iron certainty, on which he was willing to bet his career—and did.

PERSONAL EMOTION COATING THE MEMORY IS THE KEY

Like General Walters in East Berlin, Tony Bennett on stage, in front of the audience, their collective love-flamethrower blowing straight from their hearts right into his, or whatever is the emotional equivalent inside his brain, caused some brain-part to magically open. So when Tony saw Lady Gaga looking at him, her face immediately brought up her name.

From where?

Not from a regular place in his brain, with a medical name in Latin, where it was a mere category, but from that other place, where love and emotion and personal feelings are always stored, as a whole ply, where "System 1" thinking dwells. The human part. All of it just came back.

"And here is Lady Gaga!" this brain part told him, as it had told him several times before, all of which were now fully accessible again, suffused with warm emotion.

So yes, back to sleuthing.

What can you do to have access to that part of your brain? Because you can be sure you have it too—the place your memories are kept intact as entire plies, not as dispassionate, cold data to be used as fodder for science and logic, as in Value Line, or in Compustat, where CFAs graze.

WHY YOU SHOULD GO SLEUTHING

You can have access to that magic place too if you, first of all, collect the information yourself, in person, preferably by talking to informers with whom you form a personal, sympathetic connection. Or sleuth the company's products, asking customers about them. Or the machinists, yes. And the info better be personal and physical, so that your cortex can't cheat you out of a big chunk of its content, the important uncategorizable part. You want all of it, easily accessible to you, whenever you want it, before it is urgent and critical.

And your sleuthing better be done in the direction your instinct had told you was best to go; just don't ask it how it did it.

But alright, let's ask how.

HOW TO DEVELOP YOUR SLEUTHING INSTINCT OF WHICH DIRECTION TO TAKE

It did it by you giving yourself first the relevant experience. You've read the old historians, and the few good new historians, and learned to take the measure of exceptional personalities. Then you let your brain tell you which kind of personality this particular CEO resembles, and why. What are his or her flaws, and what risks do these flaws point to?

But not just the CEO and CFO and other C-Suite people. Also the lower-ranked people, the kind that Rene McPherson said were often undervalued. Give yourself leeway to gauge them as people, and let them talk. Then allow yourself to *feel* if you trust them or not—don't ask yourself why. Just let your gut tell you. And then all of it will go into the one ply that your brain, somehow, had stored, somewhere. Like Tony's brain did.

NOT JUST PEOPLE INFO

But don't just gather people info in that one company. Gather *other* companies' info, as comparable cases. Yes, like the case studies I've been presenting for you here. Then ask yourself what other company *this* one reminds you of. Or what *military* battle this *corporate* battle reminds you of. Or whether this CEO's plan reminds you of a past success, or failure, in another past company or past battle. And you can't even tell why.

Of course, know the numbers cold, like a good boy- or girl-scout CFA. You want to know what your opponents know, and do. But remember that you do it not to just imitate CFAs, but to take their money. And to do that, you must do what they don't, go where they can't, see what they don't, *feel* what they don't.

Then, over time, as the months and years roll on, even without noticing it, if you stick to Lee Kuan Yew's rule, you'll find yourself improving.

Stick how?

Coming right up.

If you go through the exercise detailed in the next, final chapter, you'll see your sleuthing skills improving before your very eyes.

CHAPTER 10
ARTISTS' POINT OF VIEW

How to get to Carnegie Hall: practicing the basics vs. your Jiminy C.

There is a famous cartoon (I think it was in the *New Yorker*), showing a man with a violin case under his arm walking down a street in New York. The man stops a passer-by and asks him how to get to Carnegie Hall.

The passer-by responds: Practice.

This advice is good for all types of performing art, yet it doesn't go far enough. In this chapter I'll show you how you can apply it to investing in general and to sleuthing in particular—both of which are performance arts too. And then this chapter will supply the far-out conclusion that most such advice omits, because most advisees don't want to hear it.

First off, though, since this is a chapter for artists in general, let's make this more specific, say to the musicians among you. (Yes, that's another analogy.) And classical musicians at that.

Did you ever play a classical musical instrument? Say a violin or a piano? Seriously played? That is, aiming to be a master performer whose name draws thousands to buy tickets to Carnegie Hall?

SERIOUS ARTISTS PRACTICE DAILY

If that's the kind of musician you aspired to be, how many hours did you practice a day? Be honest, now! One hour? Two? If so, you were not serious enough. Truly serious classical players, say Yitzhak Perlman, practice three hours a day, sometimes more. (Although much more can damage the body and is not recommended. Of course, many fanatics don't listen and just do it anyway.)

And if you did practice three hours a day, even two, what kind of things did you practice?

Say you played the violin, as per above. Did you straightaway begin to play Bach sonatas for solo violin, or Paganini caprices? On stage? With a real audience? Really?

Of course not. If you did, you'd be laughed out of the hall and never recover.

START BY PRACTICING THE BASICS

Rather, you probably started by playing exercises, aka etudes, on a beginner's violin, to learn the very basics. And if it's a violin you played, you probably started with "Wohlfahrt's 40 elementary studies," or "Otakar Sevcik violin techniques," then rose to play Kreutzer etudes, and perhaps, if you were good, graduated to Rode's 24 caprices. (Some of which, by the way, are good enough to perform with.)

And if, after a lot of daily practice, you became really good (assuming you did not damage your fingers by overplaying), only then did you graduate to Paganini.

No, no public performance yet, or maybe one, with other young violinist beginners, all of you playing together Paganini's "Motto Perpetuo," which is easier than the caprices and can be played (at half speed) after the Kreutzer etudes. But not Paganini's caprices. Not yet. And certainly not the first, nor the fifth caprice.

And it goes without saying that, even before playing Kreutzer's etudes, you had likely practiced basic bowing techniques and finger positions—the very building blocks of violin music. Just to produce an acceptable sound, before being allowed to string several sounds together.

Now why have I gone into so much detail?

Because *in every performing art there are the basics.* Whether it's violin playing, book writing, oil painting, trapeze acrobatics, stage magic, public oratory, or top-tier investing. Each such performance art has its basic techniques which you must learn, and then practice. And practice again, and again. And again.

And again.

Just like Leela played chess again and again, or Picasso copied and recopied Velasquez's "Infanta" over a full year, or Demosthenes practiced his public speaking on the sea shore, to be heard over the waves, again and again.

And again.

So must you practice investment basics until they are part of you.

But don't do them for real yet. Certainly not on the public stock-market's stage, with lots of real money, where mistakes are costly and sometime terminal. That will come. But first you must practice your art in a safe environment where you can make *correctable* mistakes, the kind that don't kill you, that you can learn from, and improve.

Improve how?

You got it: by doing more of what has worked for you, in the practice room, and doing none of what hasn't. The rest will follow, once you go real.

Yes, in investing too, practice the basics first.

But what *are* investing's basics?

Picking winning stocks is really pre-basics. It is equivalent to producing a good tone on a musical instrument. That's what beginning music players think they already do, by looking at the music notes, thinking it's all there, but of course it isn't. Like the "accounting notes" in the financial statements, music notes tell you *about* the tune, in a "System 2" sort of way. But they are not the music *itself.* That last is pure "System 1," what Tony Bennett does, as do all real musicians. They play what's *beyond* the notes.

PICKING STOCKS IS MERELY INVESTMENT TONE PRODUCTION

In my first book, *TSI,* you can find out about "investment's tone production." *TSI* was about picking *individual* stocks by sleuthing. But picking one stock is not investing. Just like Tony Bennett's holding one note is not making music, so picking and holding one stock is not good enough for an entire portfolio, which is *the investment equivalent of music—how you string the stocks together.*

Yes, you can practice individual stock-picking by sleuthing stocks again and again, and you should. Chatting with informers, learning about the CEO's character, talking to engineers about their R&D process, or even chatting with supermarket employees about which product always flies off the shelves and which stays stale. Even doing just this will teach you and give you an edge.

And if you introduce a Jay-kind-of-method into it, or Leela's, or LKY's, you'll improve steadily and extract more of a "System 1" kind of info out of your sleuthing. Just as General Walters has probably been doing all his life, talking to informers in their own languages (six of them), and as Phil Fisher has been doing in his unstructured scuttlebutt gathering, in early tech days (and documented in his great book, *Common Stocks and Uncommon Profits*).

But how much of it *can* you do? And which parts of sleuthing should you prefer, and when? How to decide? Your time is not unlimited, so you must set priorities. Else, how can you practice the basics of running a full portfolio? Of a dozen stocks? Or maybe more? (Hopefully not more). There just aren't enough hours in the days for that! What do you do first, what second, and what none at all?

The answer, of course, is Jay's method, which is also Lee Kuan Yew's method, and Leela's: you do what works, and *stop doing what doesn't.* (The latter, you'll see, is often hardest.)

But still, how to decide what works? That is, works for *you*?

HOW TO SLEUTH WELL WHILE STILL HAVING A LIFE

How can you string together a half-dozen, or a dozen well-sleuthed stocks into the equivalent of "Fly Me to the Moon," and not only make each one ring true—buying each in the right amount, the right time, the right tempo—but also do all of them together? In a well-balanced portfolio of sound? That rises, and soars, and performs? And quits at the right time, before it dies?

As the old *New Yorker* cartoon said: you must practice.

Whatever your performance art is, to get to its own Carnegie Hall you must practice it. And to practice sleuth investing you don't just sleuth a single stock, but several. Yet just how to do this, doing each thing at just the right time, as Tony Bennett knew just how long to hold a note?

How do you get into and out of several stocks, while keeping in touch with the real, non-categorized physical info behind each, while not letting it consume your life? Without consecrating your entire life to money, without becoming a priest of money, as Warren and Charlie did? How can you do this and also have some time left to live your life? With your loved ones, for whom you do all this? Because otherwise, what good to you is your money?

You can only learn it by doing it yourself, and keeping track.

If there's one thing that this book can give you, besides a few hours of fun reading for a value price, indeed what practically no other investment book does, is this: shows you how to practice your investing art.

How do I know that no other book tells you this?

FEW BOOKS TELL YOU HOW TO PRACTICE INVESTING

Because when I occasionally give talks to MBA students, none of their investment classes include practicing the entire investing art put together. While Julliard's music school stresses the importance of practicing your instrument daily, and fencing masters stress the importance of practicing basic lunges and ripostes daily, and Top Gun fighter pilots (who're artists too) fight mock sky-duels daily, almost no university investing classes teach daily practice. No investing textbook does either, nor popular books.

I know, because I have a shelfful of them. Nearly all teach picking stocks.

Almost no investment program stresses doing what Top Gun pilots do every day, every week, every month: Play mock duels with the market with fake money just as Top Gun pilots do for practice with gun cameras, which are in effect fake bullets, every day.

The best pilots in the world are those who practice the most, the Israelis. An Israeli Top Gun pilot practices 400 hours a year. An American pilot, maybe 300 hours, tops. A French one, or a Brit, perhaps 200 hours. Russians, 150 hours. Maybe.

If you practice "on dry," as they say in the army, you'll soon find what you do well, so you can do more of it "on real." Each of us is better at some things, not so good at others, while bad in a few. Me too. Thus when you practice, you'll soon discover what you do truly badly, and next time you'll do none of it. *This alone will boost your performance.* It did mine. But you must do it in surroundings which are as-real-as-possible, although also as safe as you can make them, but still scary enough to show you the What If.

Yes, the Berlitz method, writ large.

Then you can improve. Like Leela does, as per LKY's dictum. And as Jay did. And as I have. And as Top Gun pilots do. And as, I'm sure, Warren and Charlie have done, over the years, when they played with little money, and paid attention.

For example, one thing they have learned over the years is, never, never ever overpay. In the entire history of Berkshire, they have never raised their initial offer price. Not once. They always give their best price, take it or leave it.

That's something you learn if you keep track of what you do, seeing what's worked and what hasn't. Warren started with for-real money. But you don't have to.

LIKE TOP GUNS, PRACTICE FIRST "ON DRY," BUT IN REAL CONDITIONS

You can start with fake money, and as Top Guns do, train on doing it as if it's for real. As long as you want. But it better be long, and continuous, because *you, and your emotions, and your fatigue, and your mistakes, are all part of it.*

In a sidebar, you may ask, why do all these other fighter pilots, the non-Israelis, practice less?

Maybe because the others don't have a daily risk of death in real battle. Or because training on modern jet fighters is expensive, and other nations have other priorities for their money. Like beer universities, where beer masters perfect their art, as the German do. Or become master cheese makers, then take a whole summer off to bake yourself, as the French do. Or maybe because other pilots are not as driven, and so aren't focused on it. Probably all of the above.

What can this teach you about your investing practice? What should it include?

It better include taking real risks, but in a controlled surrounding, not repeating mistakes, taking notes, doing more of what works, none of what doesn't, and focus. And practicing lots. Lots. And again, and again, and again.

But practice what? Practice how?

And what's hidden here is: Why? Just to do it a bit better? To outdo Warren and Charlie?

No.

IF YOU CAN'T OUTPERFORM, STAY OUT OF THE MARKET

Remember how this book started? My aim was twofold: first, to show you why sleuthing works, so you'd do it, then show you how you can outperform the market by using this method.

But outperforming is the key. Because *if you cannot, you shouldn't be investing at all.* I am serious. If you cannot do better than the market, just buy an index fund, like Buffett recommends, or buy Berkshire stock, yes. It may lag the SPY a smidge, but it at least outperformed the bigger-capped Dow Jones (by a smidge also), which is not easy either.

But how can you tell whether *you* can outperform the market?

It's just like learning to play the violin, or learning to write fiction, or mastering Japanese bow shooting. *You have to practice the basics, daily, again and again, then advance little by little, by doing more of what works for you, and resisting doing what hasn't, and doesn't.*

Here is how you do it for investing:

START A FAKE-MONEY PORTFOLIO

1. *Start with creating a fake portfolio.* Go to finance.yahoo.com, get yourself registered with a name of your choice, and create a portfolio. Name it as per your preference, but I suggest you choose a low-key name, to induce a feeling of modesty and humility.

You are student, remember. Not a master. Yet.

Let's say the portfolio is called (your-name) SI practice-portfolio September 23 2022. (I like to put a date in the portfolio's name, to make it easy to see when it was started).

START LIKE THE FED: CREATE CASH

2. Still in finance.yahoo.com, *create a security called $$Cash*. That's your first position. Decide what size this fake portfolio will be. Make the size meaningful to you, not too low, not too high. Remember: *your reactions to the portfolio's ups and downs are part of your aim*. Like a Top Gun testing how big a g-force he/she can stand, or how rattled he/she would be, and still make the right decisions—but first testing this in a centrifuge, not in an F-15 or F-16, certainly not an F-22. So you, too, choose an amount that will give *you* real emotions when it fluctuates, if you imagine it has become real money. If you are a student, 50k is a fortune, and you may choose 25k. If older, perhaps 50k or 100k.

Or more? Your choice.

You'll then have to decide on the portfolio's currency. Here I assume it's USD, but you can choose CDN, or any other, Rupee if you want, if you invest in India, or EU, if you are a European (whatever that is). It's your portfolio, your gut-feel, and your choice.

Say you chose $100,000. You then set up the unit price as 1.00 (this will never change, since it is not a publicly traded security), and set the number of shares you have at 100,000.

HOW TO BUY A STOCK IN YOUR TRAINING PORTFOLIO

3. Now assume you want to *buy a stock* for $5,000. Say 1,000 shares of XYZ at $5.00 a share—today's offer (Ask) price. (Soon you'll see how to decide on what amount to buy.) To do that, you "sell" 5,010 "shares" of $$Cash at $1 (no gain, no loss), and buy 1,000 shares of XYZ at $5.00. ($10 is the commission.)

Your portfolio will now have a position of 94,990 shares of $$Cash at $1.00, and 1,000 shares of XYZ at $5.00. It is down by $10 already—the commission expense. (This will teach you not to overtrade.) When the markets are open, your Yahoo portfolio's value will be continuously updated, up or down. (But you'll have to add dividends manually, as additions to $$CASH.)

So is that it?

Not by a long shot. Because here comes the deep crux of it: *your financial conscience*. What I will call your Jiminy, named after Jiminy Cricket, Disney's version of the *Grillo Parlante*, Pinocchio's talking cricket.

YOUR INVESTMENT CONSCIENCE

Jiminy was an annoying little cricket that always told Pinocchio the truth. It was annoying, because Pinocchio was an habitual liar, especially to himself. He told lies to himself to avoid admitting the painful truth that he was a puppet, not a real boy. Just like you often tell lies to yourself (and to others) on how good an investor you are.

As I used to do, long ago, before I wised up.

But *you* won't, because in this training portfolio you won't be able to lie. Your market Jiminy will make your nose grow long if you do. Who or what is your Jiminy? It is a single share of SPY, or DIA, if you want. (Or, if you are a Canadian, the XIU-T, which is the ETF of the Canadian market as a whole, aka the TSX. Or the XSP-T, which is the S&P ETF in Canadian dollars.)

Say you bought 1 share of SPY, for $400.00. Since it's only for a benchmark, it's just a marker, so there's no commission. All you do is sell 400 shares of $$Cash for 1.00, and buy 1 share of SPY at $400. (Or you can buy 0.1 share at 400.00 for $40 total. It's just a marker, so you can do fractional shares, which in real life you cannot.)

From now on, the up/down moves of your Jiminy—the 1 share of SPY—will tell you whether you deserve to be in investing's Carnegie Hall or not. Or in any other kind of public investing hall. That is, *whether your daily efforts* of analysis and sleuthing and chatting with informers about the CEO and CFO, asking customers about their opinion of company XYZ's products, let alone your hours of study and mental anguish and self-doubt, *whether all this is worth the effort*. Your effort. Because, always remember, you could just have bought the SPY—or DIA—or BRK-B, yes—for the whole amount and gone to the beach with your kids, and played ball. And still outperformed 92% of everyone else in the market.

Including, perhaps, Warren and Charlie. And got a dividend too, to buy the beachball with.

Never forget that. You're in it for the performance art, yes, but *mainly you're in it for da money.*

That's why, if after a long period of fake investing (say 2-3 years—see it as investing school) you find that your portfolio, after a lot of aggravating, time-consuming activities, both sleuthing and reading the filings (yes, you have to do that), has *still* not outperformed the SPY, or the DIA, you'll have to face the bitter truth. You are *not* investing, but are just "playing stock market," a costly, make-believe video game that costs you time and money but *has no monetary value.*

IF YOU CAN'T BEAT THE MARKET, DON'T BE IN IT

You don't like what I am saying? Tough. Just see me as your volunteer Jiminy C. I am telling you the bald truth. It's better to be offended by it here, in the privacy of our get-together over coffee, without any cost to you except to your pride (and the price of the book, and the coffee), than having your financial nose chopped off for real by the stock market, which might mean you'll have to become a barista.

Which, if the losses are only in your fake portfolio, wouldn't be necessary.

Sure, being told the truth may cost your ego dearly, as Top Guns training often does to pilots (they have psychologists to help the struggling ones get over it), but it will help you save time and money, both of which you can then consecrate to what you are *really* good at.

On the other hand:

If you track what *doesn't* work for you as well as what *does,* and act on both, continuously, it can make you richer over time, perhaps much richer, *if you find that you do have what it takes.*

Because you just might, you know. And you'll never know it if you don't try it, as Top Guns do.

Well then. You have just loaded your training portfolio with fake-money—that's your gun camera—and are ready to go on a test dog-fight against Mr. Market.

It will be a long trial-fight—I suggest 2 to 3 years—but that's up to you.

Let's go, then.

STRINGING SLEUTHED STOCKS TOGETHER

4. *Pick a stock.* How? See my first book. Start with a stock with a high Q and a high V (see a list of 15 in Appendix 1), or a turnaround (not recommended), or any other stock you think worthwhile. You decide. Write down *why* you chose this one (besides its appearance here). The main reasons, in order of priorities—and give this order some thinking. You should sleuth the stock by *this* order of priorities, if possible. Dedicate more time to the important priorities, less to the less. How do you know which is which? Well, you start by using "System 2" thinking: logic. But as you start sleuthing, you'll see that *the order of priorities changes as you investigate.* And it'd better! As you learn *physical* facts from *real* life, you'll realize that what you'd gathered from ink and bits by mere "System 2" logic wasn't the *whole* truth. Now, as you sleuth, your "System 1" instinct comes into play, and suddenly you see more deeply into the situation. And before you know it, you are on your way.

Next: How many of these priority points are public? How many of your private facts, based on your sleuthing are? Mark it down! Then as you go on and improve, this ratio had better go up. How will you know this? *Because you'll write down everything you do,* as well as your conclusions, during this long dog-fight simulation. See it as your detailed log book, like the one all pilots keep.

Something like: Date: dd/mm/yy. Stock: XYZ. Exceptional company (found it myself) as per its Q, not so cheap on its V (since EV/EBITDA is high). Reasons for exceptionality: Reason 1, Reason 2, Reason 3. Sleuthed first by talking to regional manager's assistant (three weeks to get introduced, one week to make contact), two stevedores on the loading dock, a customer's buyer, and a clerk in City Hall where XYZ is building a big new facility. Seems to be delayed. Why? No one knows yet, but barman across City Hall says there are rumors. What rumors? Find out! Call who? Town newspaper maybe? Or barman again? Idea: go to City Council meeting, chat with councillors in diner across City Hall. Later: XYZ's new CEO reminds me (via councillors' stories) of Lysander the Spartan who conquered Athens by a trick. Wily and persistent and underestimated, say some. Holding up construction for better deal from city. May even get it. Also: XYZ's main competitors seem half asleep, based on their salesmen

(I called two, pretending to be a potential customer), but the sharper one is wary of XYZ's "new products." What are they? Check them out. How? Option 1, option 2. Or wait until they are in beta stage? Meantime: Check CEO's background, worked once in ABC Co's engineering dept. See if I can get introduced to someone there via my buddy Mike, who lived in ABC HQ's small town.

Then you write: Should wait a while, even though new products very good, say engineer buddy, to buy stock only under $15, to bring V into buyable range. (Or, a year later, you write: Waiting has been a mistake. Stock zoomed, without me.) Or, you now write: Pass on XYZ stock because of reasons a, b, and c. Or: Everything looks good, except d and e are risks. Sleuth these out before deciding. Sleuth how? Idea 1, idea 2. May have to get contacts inside XYZ's main client. How? Idea 1, idea 2, idea 3. Which is best? Why? NB: Idea 1 seems good, but twice before has proved a waste of time, probably because reason 1 and reason 2. So try Idea 2 first.

Half these notes, as you can see, are *Sleuthing Projects you give yourself*, like Jay, or like a research director in an investing boutique gives his or her analysts. Therefore, like that RD, you must *prioritize projects*. That's the second lesson you'll learn, after learning to *prioritize topics*. It's a good lesson for life too. You can't do everything. Specialize, prioritize, delegate. Yes, even delegate your investing to Warren and Charlie (or the SPY, or the DIA) if you have to.

But maybe you *wouldn't* have to?

YOUR MARCHING ORDERS AND DISPATCHES FROM THE FRONT, ALL IN ONE

Because all these notes will most likely help you in the later Lee Kuan Yew stage, when you try to improve by doing more of what *has* worked, and less (or none) of what *hasn't—as documented by your notes*. Just as Jay learned to sell better, or Leela how to win in chess, this note-taking and follow-upping will also teach you what *not* to do. For example, say you had waited to buy on a "chart signal," which later proved to be nonsense. This will teach you in future to ignore charts. Things like that.

In other words, *your notes will become part of your Jiminy C's voice.* Jay's Jiminy was his notebook (in Hindi). Leela's, her capacious memory. Your memory is not as large, but—that's another uncomfortable truth—even if it were, *you couldn't trust it, because it would remember your successes but forget your failures,* just to protect you against feeling bad. That's why your notes are essential. Trust me on this. I've been there.

5. Now decide on the *tranche size* (aka position size). Before buying, you must decide how much of the new stock to buy—what % of your portfolio (and your mind share, see below) it should be. If you talk to pro investors, you'll find that the *tranche size* is what they often discuss. It can be anywhere between 1% and 20%. Traders (who mostly stare glumly at their screen) often use 1% or 2%. In my experience, long-term investors use 5 to 8%, or, rarely, 10%. Only active fixit (turnaround) investors who get involved in the company's operations invest more than 10%. But then they invest their time. And how much is that worth? How much is yours? Please see more about it below.

Now why is the tranche's % of your portfolio important?

Because if it's too small, your brilliant pick won't matter much, like Warren Buffett's $950 billion portfolio barely moving on a "mere" $9.5 billion new investment. Also, by choosing too small a tranche, you'd be slicing away your sleuthing time (and mindshare) into small pieces. That is your scarcest resource. Don't fritter it.

On the other hand, if the tranche is too big, say 20 or 30%, then a loss can wipe you out for several years. Or even if not a loss, just the fluctuation may stress you emotionally, like extreme g-forces do for a pilot—and your peace of mind is valuable. That's why Buffett said that "temperament" for an investor is more important than IQ. You can't change your IQ (although that's somewhat arguable, if you train hard), but you *can* improve your temperament by exercising it, as you are doing now. Or at least testing its limits.

THE "OUCH POINT"

What you're looking for here is your ouch point. At what point does your lizard brain (part of "System 1") slither into its black hole and scream:

"Let's get out of here! I don't care how, I don't care at what price, because I'm scared! Sell-sell-sell!"?

You can find this high-g point in real life by paying through the nose, à la Pinocchio. Or you can pay with pride only, in a fake portfolio such as this, where you'll learn it through the LKY-Jay-Berlitz method, and your annoying Jiminy C (the SPY share) and the portfolio drawdown—the peak-to-trough plunge of your portfolio.

For example, you may think (via your "System 2") that you can take a -30% drawdown. But in real life, with real money, even -15% drawdown may cause you to sell, and -20% may cause you a real panic, and I mean a physical one, yes.

As a reminder: the October 1987 crash, which left lots of human wetness on trading room floors worldwide, was -23.5% in one day. I know, because I was there. That's the second time I saw several grown men shed tears of fear. (The first was in a real shooting war.)

NOTE TO YOURSELF: YOUR PORTFOLIO IS A CARGO-PLANE, *NOT* A FIGHTER-JET

6. Now your mock-market battle begins: there are many stock targets out there, and you keep an eye on several. Some are soaring, others plunging, either their EPS engines spluttered or just air pockets. There are also other investor-pilots around, both funds and gurus, flying large portfolios, and huge flocks of amateurs like you. Some fly small cargo planes carrying stocks long distance, but most fly tiny fighter planes, usually in the wake of gurus. They're taking pot shots at passing stocks and at other portfolio-planes, chortling on Twitter as they buy and sell, telling all the world about their doings. Occasionally a fighter jet portfolio goes down in flames. That's a trader shot down by another. Eventually you notice that the faster a portfolio plane goes, the more likely it is to be shot down. Slow cargo planes are safest. All cargo planes fly close to the market plane, the SPY, which is the hugest, and yet seems the fastest, even though it crawls along and falls into air-pockets just like all others. Very few outfly it in front, most are behind. Especially the trading fighter-planes. Whichever of them still flies, that is, because most blow up and plunge, only a few rising again, patched up with fresh money, which they constantly shed.

Lots going on. Lots of excitement. Lots to watch.

What *should you* watch, then, outside your portfolio? Other stocks? Gurus? The economic winds?

DECISIONS, DECISIONS—WHICH SHOULD YOU MAKE, WHICH NOT?

7. So here is a word from your flight instructor: it's best to focus on your own portfolio, the stocks in it, and the decisions you'll have to make—or not make. Here are the main ones: keep a detailed logbook of your decisions, and why you made them, and what was the result. Over time you'll see what works for you, and what doesn't.

In no particular order, these are some of the decisions:

- Which stock to buy? (See my first book, *TSI*, as well as chapter 7.)
- How much % of the portfolio in any one stock? (See above, in 5.)
- How much in *this* particular stock? (See the part in chapter 3 about confidence due to sleuthing, but also max drawdown you can stand—the portfolio "g-force.")
- Why do you want to buy this stock? (See above about a prioritized list.)
- When would you sell it? (Key factors, prioritized.) Why this order? (Ditto.)
- What % of the portfolio should you keep in cash? (Here, you are on your own.)
- If you like a new stock more than others, should you sell the least-attractive stock that you own, to buy the new one? (Again, you are on your own here. But see the constraint of maintenance time and mind share, below.)
- When should you add to a stock you like? When it rises? Or when it falls? And under what conditions? (Again, you are on your own, but keep a record.)

- When to sell a stock if it becomes a "too high % of the portfolio"? What're the decision criteria? Think carefully about this. In advance.

- What if a stock throws a big surprise? What if you find management lied? What if you find you love a stock, but a famous guru hates it? What if it's the opposite?

- How to track your Jiminy if you add money to the portfolio? The answer: just buy more such ETF in proportion to the money you added, at the-then market price.

All these (and more) are questions you'll face continuously in your fake-money simulation, and will have to decide how many of them (and which) are important. After a year or so you'll have enough data to see which (and how many) such questions you answered, how you answered them, and *whether the answers mattered or not.*

That last point is very important, because most likely *you'll see that you are making too many decisions*, agonizing over low priorities, and worrying overmuch about the short term. The aim is to make fewer decisions, but important ones for the long term, so that you can *dedicate as much time as you can to physical sleuthing.*

Equally important, you'll discover what you are *not* good at, in black and white, so the evidence in your own logbook would not fail to convince you to *just not do it.* And, as you'll discover, this often gives the quickest payoff. It also leaves you more time for doing what are good at—and also more time for beachball with the kids. It worked for me. (I have two.)

WHAT DOES AND WHAT DOESN'T WORK FOR ME

What did *I* learn that does not work for me?

Oh, where to start?

One of the first things I learned is that I should never buy or sell options. I am not good enough to compete against D.E. Shaw, whose computers price options within a fraction of a penny. Worse, doing options forces you into short-term thinking, which is mental poison for sleuths.

Right after options (for me), comes mining stocks. I can't invest in them profitably enough to justify my time and effort. I know it's shameful (for a Canadian) to admit, but sleuthing mine ore deposits and chatting to miners in the bush is just not in my skillset. On the other hand, I have skilled (Canadian) friends who do nothing but mines, and they excel at it. I realized that if I wanted to invest in mining stocks, I should let them do it for me. This leaves me time for Tech stocks, which I love, and for large Q,V situations, and the odd turnaround (my weakness).

Or how about insiders' buying and selling, as an indicator that a stock may be worth sleuthing? As you probably know, an insider of a public company who either buys or sells shares of his company must report it, so that you and me (and everyone else) can see it. Most investors use all such info as a useful indicator. Long ago I thought so too.

But is it really? It is useful, but not all of it, and not always, as my logbook shows.

Over the years I found that some insiders are far better than others at buying and selling their own shares at just in the right time, while other insiders make mistakes. Who are the most prescient ones? The problem is, they vary from company to company.

If you want to find out, track the insiders of the companies you have sleuthed, by name and by job function, and over time you'll see for yourself.

Another thing I found to my shame is that I should not spend my time on turnarounds. I am not bad, really. But the effort involved is often disproportionate to the profit potential. Do I invest in turnaround stocks anymore? Shamefully, I must admit I occasionally do, because, like Carl Icahn, I like the drama. (I even turned around one company myself long ago.) But these days I put smaller amounts into such situations, because it's often like writing a free call on my time. If you, like me, like turn-around situations, be forewarned…

WHAT ARE YOU NOT GOOD AT?

Now, do you know what areas of the market *you* are not good at? Just by asking the question you are already far ahead, because once you know this and don't do it, you won't lose money. And then you'll have time to ask the opposite question: What are you truly good at? What comes to you naturally? And what's your *evidence* that you really are so?

Don't look for me to give you this answer. It will be in your fake-portfolio's log book. And it may surprise you. For all you know, you have nose for turnarounds, and are a whiz in mining stocks. Or maybe not. Maybe you too dislike mining stocks but love biotech? One thing is certain: your experience is different than mine, and so is your skill set. Yes, in some ways we are all the same, but in others, all different.

8. Now what of watching the market in general? To see if it is up or down? Strong or weak? Bullish or bearish? So as to see whether you should trade in or out of a stock?

Now this is your post-flight instructor speaking:

A good first rule is *don't watch the market too much*. And a good second rule is, *don't play dog-fight, which is trading*. Keep your eye on your long-term goal—the Rich City (called retirement) shining on the hill (where the SPY is aiming also), and on your own portfolio plane, in which you carry preciously sleuthed stocks. Keep your attention on them, smell them often, to see if they have gone stale, look into their eyes and ask how they are doing, not into the dozen Internet screens showing the fun dogfight outside, or you'll be tempted to turn your cargo plane into a trading jet. Like the ones being shot down every minute.

Besides: Remember your peace of mind? The screen will kill it, as will the continuous effort to overcome temptation to trade.

RATIO OF SLEUTHING TIME TO INTERNET TIME IS KEY

And, let me stress this once more. Keep a logbook of what goes on, both inside and outside, if you must: what happened, what you did then, why, and what was the result. Once you are back on base—that's after market hours—you can analyse it: What were you really spending time on? And why? Track how much of it was spent on Twitter with a coffee nearby, how much on physical data you produced yourself, without any A.C. around. In my experience, *the ratio of non-A.C.-sleuthing time to Internet time is key*. The higher it is, the better the results. On almost any aspect of the company. (I said 'almost.') Feel free to use Jay's method to test *variations* of what works for you, and what doesn't. Especially in dealing with people. (It'll help you also in your private life, by the way. But that's just by the by.)

9. Once a month or so, note your mistakes. Explicitly. In newspaper reporter style: what, where, why, when, who (who is obviously you, but also who lied to you, etc.) See if there's any pattern. Anything you should do less of? Anything more of? Even if it is not obvious why? Remember: you are after *correlation*, not *causation*; like Leela and Jay. You don't care too much *why* something works. Only that it *does*. (However, the Why would usually be obvious.)

10. Note especially *how long* it took you to do *all* of this, and *individual parts* of it. Both the buy/sell, and the tracking and ongoing sleuthing. Because *once you own a stock, you have to keep track of the company behind it, physically*. Therefore, one of the key Buy criteria of a stock, is *how intense would be its sleuthing maintenance*. Which includes reading the filings, on top of the sleuthing. Owning a stock is like a friendship/relationship. Best is long-term, beneficial, and with low-to-medium maintenance. Not zero, just low-to-mid. You can bring it flowers once a month, but not a mink coat once a week. So if maintenance time on a stock is high and rising, beyond a certain point, rethink the ownership. You can do better with your time. A stock is not a human, to which you owe allegiance. It certainly is not family. (Hint: high Q,V stocks often need less maintenance.)

CORRELATION BETWEEN YOUR ERRORS AND LOW PERFORMANCE

11. Once a year, see if you have done better than the market (that's your Jiminy C), and by how much. If you haven't—why not? What caused your biggest drag on performance? Too big a tranche? Too fast a decision to buy? Impatience to hold? Missed a corporate deterioration because you haven't spent physical sleuthing time after you'd bought the stock? Why didn't you? In my experience, one of the biggest failures is *overreacting because you didn't know enough, physically*, since you didn't sleuth enough; especially the most important thing. Because you didn't know it was. So you panicked, which you wouldn't have—indeed, you could have seen the plunge as an opportunity, if you'd only known that particular fact.

TIME SQUEEZE THE RESULT OF TOO MANY STOCKS—OR WRONG PRIORITIES

Many such errors happen *because you've gotten into a time-squeeze.* And have you? Welcome to the club. That's a common problem for starting sleuths. They fall in love with the process because of the quick improvements it often brings, like the keto diet. So they do more of *everything* about it, instead of picking and choosing the most important pieces, i.e., they *fall into the trap of consecrating their life to money*, as Perlman does to violin playing (by his own admission.) But then, for him it's worth it. You are not the Perlman of stocks.

Or are you?

Your Jiminy C will help you find out. That, and your notes. So write it all down. This, too, will be part of the periodic LKY fixit actions. (And yes, such note-taking is time consuming too.)

12. Finally, if you *do* manage to outdo the market (as eventually you might, with a much higher than 8% chance, just by eliminating your main errors), note this outperformance and what it's likely due to. But *don't spend too much time on the Why. You can only know it approximately*, and, remember, you're looking for *correlation, not causation.* You are *not* a scientist here.

HIGHER LEVEL OF TOUGH LOVE

Then, once you're at long last at (somewhat) faster-than-SPY speed, what can you do? Here you should engage in a higher-level tough-love exercise. Say you outperform the market by, oh, 3% per year (not easy), how much is this in dollars, for the size of your portfolio? Here (for $100K) it would be $3K per year. So how much is it per hour of your toil, instead of being in the SPY, or in BRK/B?

This brings up an even less palatable truth than the one revealed by Jiminy C.

JC only tells you *whether* you have outperformed the market. *It doesn't tell you whether it is worth your time.* Assume that your overperformance, at your $100K portfolio size, is the above $3K per year but you've spent 10 hours per week (2 hours per day, no weekends, which are for beachball with the kids), on 50 weeks a year (2 for vacation), or 250 hours a year. This comes up to $12/hour, or barely minimum wage.

Hmmm…

You're almost certainly being paid more in your day job, or reading this book would likely be beyond you.

So: Is it worth it?

It is, *if* you make the following assumptions:

a. The 100k will grow, so soon it would be more than that per hour—and accumulate.

b. Your experience will grow, so the 3% over-the-market gain could grow too. Especially when you eliminate mistakes. Like acting on charts, or gurus' tips, or Wall Street Buys.

c. You enjoy sleuthing-and-winning more than golf, and it costs less, also with JC you can't lie.

d. Tracking what you do prevents you from losing money, because it shows you what's foolish.

e. If you run not $100K, but $1 million, the extra gain is $30K p.a., not $3K, or $120 per hour. And if it's $10 million, then it's $1,200 an hour more, which begins to prove the value of sticking to it.

f. You aim to run lots of OPM as a money manager, so if you can prove (to OPM owners) that you can grow it at trans-SPY speed (aka Alpha), they'll pay you liberally, and both you and they will be far ahead. Which was the case for Warren and Charlie, up to fifteen years ago.

WHAT IF YOU ARE IMPATIENT?

13. But what if you say you can't stop "investing" for so long and just practice, because:

1. you fear missing the gains you could make via your Internet investing, or
2. what if all this fake-portfolio practice doesn't work for you?

The answer is simple:

If you insist on continuing "investing" as you've done up to now—which hasn't enabled you to beat the market, remember—who I am to stop you?

But at least also do this:

As you continue to "invest" via "Internet info," please also invest *on the side* some "fake money" in a training portfolio, as per the above instructions, but *strictly on real info you sleuth yourself.*

You don't have to fake-invest in many stocks, just in those you sleuthed yourself, as per the methods you've found in this book and in its predecessor, *TSI.*

THEN COMPARE YOUR OWN RESULTS TO YOUR FAKE-PORTFOLIO'S

If you do that, then in a year, or two, compare your training-portfolio's results to your real-money results. I am very confident that you'll have to admit sheepishly that your "Internet investing" has still not managed to keep up either with the market, i.e., the SPY, or with your fake-money investing in well-sleuthed stocks.

And I know of what I speak.

I've done this many years ago, and I can still feel the blow to my ego when I realized that 80% of my investing activity was detrimental to my profits. Ever since, I've always had a few test fake-portfolios running alongside my real ones, where I am testing ideas over time, to see what's working and what isn't. Not just in theory but in practice.

How did I get the notion to do this?

As an aeronautical engineer, I always understood that critical components must undergo stress testing in the lab, before being incorporated into the final design. If something was going to break, it should break on the ground first, so the final component can be designed with a high margin of safety. (A term later incorporated into value investing by Seth Klarman of Baupost.)

This was true for airplane wings, rocket engines, and key control systems in both planes and the particle accelerator, in whose design I later participated. So as practical scientist, I learned very early that nothing goes operational before it's tested to breaking point. And tested again, and again, and again.

And again.

So that's how I eventually got the idea for testing investment methods, first in the fake portfolio "lab," with myself—the portfolio's "pilot" so to speak—as part of the test, just as you'll be part of yours. And yes, as Jay was part of his system, and Leela part of hers.

You, too, should test your investing system, with you as its "pilot," to find out what works for *you* and what doesn't, and only then use it with real money.

Not back-testing, but *forward*-testing.

That is also how I chanced on the Q and V Evaluating Functions, and on the R&D value functions for tech turnarounds (see in *TSI*), and on a few others. All these work for me.

Would they also work for you?

WHAT WORKS FOR YOU MAY BE DIFFERENT—SO TEST IT

I think they would, but don't take my word for it, test them and see. *You* are part of *your* investing process, just as I am part of mine. I may have some skills and instincts (and experience) that you don't have, but then *you* almost certainly have several that *I* don't.

Yes, again like Jay's instinct, and Leela's, and Lee Kuan Yew's—and yes, Warren's and Charlie's. All have different skills and instincts and experiences that work for *them*.

What are yours that work for you? You'll never know until you test them—and yourself.

But do it in the fake-portfolio lab first, *before* you climb on stage at the Carnegie Hall of investing, which of course is the stock market. But yes, you can also do it *alongside*. Run a fake test-portfolio in tandem with your real one. Your choice.

SWEAT SAVES YOU BLOOD—AND SLEUTHING SAVES YOU FROM LOSSES

Yes, doing all this involves work. But as the saying went in my army days: "Sweat saves blood." That is: hard training and practice before battle, help keep you safe in real war. And, as you'll see, as a sleuth investor one of your larger risks is cutting corners, viewing the 3-D world of commerce only through the 2-D internet slot, coffee in one hand, the other "playing stock market" video-game. Buy-sell, click-click.

All under a comfy air conditioner, no hot sweat.

However, if you keep doing that, you're likely to sweat plenty *later*—cold sweat—when sleuths like me, or Mr. Market (the SPY) take your money.

Which sweat do you prefer?

Like in war, in the market too, hot sweat now can save you from cold sweat later. It can also help you take the money of those who haven't read the book.

And *then* you'll outperform.

Now before you ask, let me repeat what I said in the intro:

NO FEAR THAT EVERYONE WILL OUTPERFORM

Am I not afraid that *everyone* will now become an experienced sleuth and so will make it much more difficult for me to make money in the market by sleuthing?

The answer is a double no. First, just as I said in *TSI*, and in the intro to this book, many readers will still find it inconvenient to turn off the Internet and go do physical sleuthing. Now many will find it doubly difficult to practice every day, for a year, or two, or more, before they go and fight it out with Mr. Market (and me and my ilk) only after discovering what really works for them and what doesn't. (Hint: fighter-jet-style trading doesn't.) Like Jay did (in sales), and Leela (in chess.) Or Lee Kuan Yew (in city-state start-up.)

EVERY SLEUTH INVESTOR'S VIEW IS DIFFERENT—BUT STILL VALID

But second, as per Niels Bohr, and Einstein (which I also noted in the intro), *every measuring-observer's view is equally valid, and so is every sleuth investor's*. Public info that CFAs use is incomplete, just as classical physics' view is incomplete. Each sleuth complements the *public* info by creating *private, new info* in the category of his or her choice. So *each sleuth can outperform the market, in his or her own way*.

What if everyone becomes a sleuth? Can everyone outperform?

IF ALL SLEUTHS ARE ABOVE AVERAGE, HOW MANY CAN THERE BE?

Again, as per the intro: this brings up shades of the mythical Lake Wobegone village, where everyone is above average. Who, then, would be below it? Whose money could you (or I) take? But we need not worry. There are always other market villages woefully *below* average, full of lazy investors who do not want to leave the house, and their coffee, to sleuth for physical info. Or yes, classical physicists who subscribe to reductionism, and insist that squiggles tell it all about the universe—and about the market. Well, their money is fair game, too. Just like yours and mine. All of us can strap ourselves into our portfolio cockpit, our fingers on the trigger, and imagine ourselves stock market Top Guns.

But are we? Are you one? You think?

REAL STOCK TOP GUNS FLY CARGO, NOT FIGHTER JETS

You probably aren't, because *the real Top Guns fly cargo portfolios*, not trading fighter-jets. They are the ones who *survive* and arrive at Retirement City a few weeks, or months, or (if they are good) several years before the SPY does. The fighter-jet trading portfolios usually blacken the desert sands, and their former pilots are now baristas serving coffee.

Are you potentially one such?

Just to make sure you aren't, go do the centrifuge first, and the simulator, which is what this chapter provides you with. Invest fake money for a year or two (or three: see it as a Top Gun academy). Use LKY's/Leela's/Jay's method on the CFA info plus your privately sleuthed info, and over time find out what you are *really* good at, and what you aren't.

Then do more of the first, and none of the second.

Found this out already, you say? So fast?

Oh, you say you don't really need to?

Just to make sure, before you strap into your real-money portfolio, come join me at the little Starbucks in Silicon Valley where I've been gossiping with a chip designer at XYZ Corp., about his employer.

What do we gossip about, you ask?

Oh, I'm told that XYZ's founder's niece (a director by inheritance) has just changed product policy to help prevent ice-cap melting, at the expense of R&D budgets. Which is why the chip designer has just resigned, with half his team about to follow.

So before you strap in: Don't you think it's significant? Based on my years of tracking what works for me and what doesn't, I think it is.

You disagree? Why?

I see. You say XYZ's chart looks good?

Fine. I'll meet you then at 9:30 on the Market's open, at the bid-ask spread.

Bring your coffee.

Toronto, October 2022

THE ADVANCED SLEUTH INVESTOR'S 12 RULES

1. **Investing is not science.** Science is a public philanthropic activity; investing is selfish and secretive. So: sleuth for private physical info and keep what you find to yourself.

2. **Not all info can be contained in squiggles**, both in science and in investing. Proven. That's why sleuth investors learn physically what intellectual "investors" never know.

3. **Modern science found the active observer is key**. A sleuth investor, too, is an active observer who creates private info. Be one and you'll take the money of the passive.

4. **Don't invest until you're trained.** Run a fake training portfolio to find what you are really good at, what bad at. Then do more of the first and none of the second.

5. **Understand the difference between a principal and an agent.** Aim to be the first type.

6. **Your brain's cortex translates all info into categories**, dropping the untranslatable Dark Info into your older brain. Access it, and you'll take the money of those who can't.

7. **Accounting is blind** to: people, unquantifiable corporate attributes, and all Dark Info that cannot be put into ink or bits. So if you get this Info, you'll take the accountants' money.

8. **Ownership has three parts:** benefit, control, and transferability. If you don't understand this, you can't get really rich, because you'll "invest" in what you don't truly own.

9. **Hire real domain experts** with long experience. Don't try to duplicate it. Pay up.

10. **Seek opinions of low- and mid-level workers** about their bosses and the company. They see and hear more than you think and know a lot, yet no one talks to them. You should.

11. **Leaders make things happen.** But they come in many varieties. Study these. There's a time and place for a Wellington, as well as for a Napoleon. You decide which is it now.

12. **Focus on the long term,** resist trading, and restrict yourself to the truly exceptional. Life is too short to waste on the mediocre. Learn to say no and wait. It's hard, but it pays big.

APPENDICES

APPENDIX 1

A sample of 15 stocks with high company quality indicator (Q), and high stock value indicator (V). This list is *not* of stocks worth buying, but of stocks worth sleuthing. (The market ETFs and BRK-A are provided as reference. We'll check all prices again in 10 years.)

	Quality	Value	03-Oct-22
Symbol	Q	V	Price (ref)
MSFT	101.6	5.9	$240.74
INMD	119.4	11.9	$30.23
CNI	88.5	9.4	$112.82
CNW	120.4	7.6	$159.91
VICI	142.7	3.5	$30.54
MEDP	78.6	4.1	$160.80
V	126.1	6.2	$181.65
FNV	82.3	4.7	$122.28
MA	259.2	11.2	$301.27
CPRT	84.0	5.1	$109.65
LULU	90.3	4.2	$292.10
ATKR	154.5	55.2	$82.18
ROST	42.9	3.2	$85.96
TJX	64.3	4.4	$62.90
JNJ	54.6	3.5	$163.20
SPY	NA	NA	$366.61
DIA	NA	NA	$294.79
BRK-A	NA	NA	$413,300.00
XIU.TO	NA	NA	$28.91

APPENDIX 2

A NOTE ABOUT RENAISSANCE TECHNOLOGIES

I've said nothing in this book about Jim Simons' Renaissance Technologies, the one hedge fund that has outperformed the market splendidly for years, without physical human sleuthing, just by using computers. However, it's well known that Ren Tech's computers use *non-finance info* also, much of it of *physical* facts (in squiggle format, yes) *external* to the financial statements. Info like atmospheric data, politics, traffic patterns, satellite images, natural disasters, commodities data and CVs of executives (allegedly), and goodness knows what else, then correlating all of this with "buy/sell success." Just like Leela, or yes, like Jay, Ren Tech's computers try this, then that, and also a bit of the other, not caring about why, only about whether it works or not, then do more of what works and skip what doesn't— and unlike chess, these two may change over time. What's significant about its process is that Ren Tech does it *continuously*, so in effect it *simulates a giant Neural Net in continuous learning mode* of The Game of Stocks. However, because what Ren Tech does cannot help *you* outperform the market, its topic is outside the scope of this book. Perhaps in the next one.

FURTHER READING

BOOKS

Gödel's Proof
Ernest Nagel, James R. Newman, Douglas R. Hofstadter (Editor and foreword: Douglas R. Hofstadter)

Common Sense, the Turing Test, and the Quest for Real AI
Hector J Levesque

On Intelligence
Jeff Hawkins

A Thousand Brains
Jeff Hawkins

The Rules of Double-Entry Bookkeeping: Particularis de computis et scripturis
Luca Pacioli

Gifts Differing: Understanding Personality Type
Isabel Briggs Myers and Peter B. Myers

Coup d'État: A Practical Handbook
Edward N. Luttwak

The Prince
Niccolò Machiavelli

Discourses on Livy
Niccolò Machiavelli

The Little Book That Beats the Market
Joel Greenblatt

Strategikon
Emperor Maurice

The Six-Month Fix
Gary Sutton

Corporate Turnaround
Donald B. Bibeault

God & Golem Inc.
Norbert Weiner

Behind Deep Blue: Building the Computer That Defeated the World Chess Champion
Feng-Hsiung Hsu (foreword: Jon Kleinberg)

Game Changer: AlphaZero's Ground breaking Chess Strategies and the Promise of AI
Matthew Sadler & Natasha Regan

Surfaces and Essences
Douglas Hofstadter and Emmanuel Sander

Parallel Lives of the Noble Greeks and Romans
Plutarch

Think on Your Feet
Keith Spicer

Common Stocks and Uncommon Profits
Philip A. Fisher

One Up On Wall Street
Peter Lynch

The Education of a Speculator
Victor Niederhoffer

Reminiscences of a Stock Operator
Edwin Lefèvre (Foreword: William J. O'Neil)

Fiat Money Inflation in France
Andrew Dickson White

Dance of the Money Bees
Adam Smith

What Works on Wall Street
James O'Shaughnessy

The Sleuth Investor
Avner Mandelman

The Advanced Sleuth Investor
Avner Mandelman

The Intelligent Investor
Benjamin Graham

Security Analysis
Benjamin Graham and David Dodd

Books about Warren Buffett and Berkshire Hathaway:

The Snowball: Warren Buffett and the Business of Life
Alice Schroeder

Warren Buffett and the Interpretation of Financial Statements: The Search for the Company with a Durable Competitive Advantage
Mary Buffett and David Clark

The Essays of Warren Buffett: Lessons for Corporate America
Lawrence A. Cunningham and Warren E. Buffett

Berkshire Hathaway Letters to Shareholders, 2021
Warren Buffett and Max Olson

PAPERS

The Unreasonable Effectiveness of Mathematics in the Natural Sciences
Eugene Wigner

Programming a Computer for Playing Chess
Claude Elwood Shannon, 1949

A Chess-Playing Machine
Claude Elwood Shannon, 1950

Hidden variables, Bell's inequality, non locality: Look up papers about them on ArXiv.org.
Neural Networks papers by Geoff Hinton—look them up on ArXiv

Neural Networks Papers by Naftali Tishby—ditto. Especially about "information bottleneck."

Sur La Theorie de Speculation / Henry Bachelier. Suggested random-walk / Brownian motion in stocks, not just in gas molecules. Einstein used the concept for his paper on the photovoltaic effect, for which he won his Nobel Prize. (No, he didn't win it for E=mc2.)

VIDEOS ON SLEUTH INVESTING

The YouTube Sleuth Investor Channel
https://www.youtube.com/channel/UCYqoVE89bEiKmybAlnLEq4w

GLOSSARY OF SOME FINANCIAL AND INVESTMENT TERMS:

P/E: Price/Earnings ratio. A measure of a stock's priciness. High is expensive, low is cheap. It can also be seen as the number of years you have to wait to get your purchase price back, if the current earnings per share persist. A high P/E obviously assumes expectations of rising earnings.

EV: Enterprise Value. Market capitalization plus all debt less cash. It shows how much you'd have to spend to own the entire company at the current market price, paying off its net debt.

EVA: Economic Value Added. A measure of a company's financial performance based on how much real excess wealth it creates, by subtracting its total cost of capital from its operating profit, after cash taxes. EVA is aka as economic profit.

EBIT: Earnings Before Interest and Taxes.

EBITDA: Earnings Before Interest, Taxes, Depreciation and Amortization. Aka owner's cash flow.

EV/EBITDA: A measure of a company's expensiveness if you want to own it all and pay off all its debt. Aka owner's valuation.

WC: Working Capital, equal to current assets less current liabilities.

Net-Net Working Capital, aka Net-NetWorking Capital less all liabilities.

EPS: Earnings Per Share.

BV: Book Value. Same as owner's equity. The accountant's value of the assets less all debt.

BV/share: Same as above, per share.

P/BV: Ratio of current Price to the accountant's Book Value.

Debt/Equity: How much the company owes, divided by the Book Value. Shows financial risk.

CF: Cash Flow. How much cash the company generates per whatever period it is given for. It is different than earnings because of some non-cash deductions, like depreciation and amortization (and also others.)

FCF : Free Cash Flow. Excess cash flow not needed in the business. Also known as cash generation.

P/CF: Price to Cash Flow. Similar to P/E, but more rigorous.

P/FCF: Price to Free Cash Flow. Similar to the above, but more rigorous still.

FCF/EV: Free Cash Flow as a percent of the Enterprise Value. Aka as owner's FCF yield.

GM: Gross Margins. Sales less the direct cost of production, the latter often explained (simplistically) as the cost of sand and glue in the production of bricks. Gross Margins are usually expressed as a percentage of sales.

ROE: Return On Equity. Earnings divided by BV. (Or, occasionally, average BV for the period.)

ROC: Return On Capital. Usually it is EBIT divided by a combination of capital and debt.

Bid-Ask spread: Stocks trading has two prices, the Ask price (aka the Offer) and the Bid price. When the stock is illiquid (not many shares trade), the difference between the Bid and the Ask is wide, so the real cost of trading is not just the commission, but the Bid-Ask spread.

Market capitalization: Number of shares times the latest stock price. It is equivalent to how much you'd have to pay for all the company shares at the current price.

Big caps, mid caps, small caps, micro caps: Stocks are divided into the size of their total market capitalizations.

ETF: Exchange Tradable Funds. It's a basket of stocks that trade together on the exchange as one stock, to mimic the activity of this collection of stocks.

SPY: The ETF that tries to replicate the movement of the S&P500.

DIA: The ETF that tries to replicate the movement of the Dow Jones Industrial Average.

S&P500: The index that tracks the average prices of 500 of the largest cap stocks. Every now and then a stock is taken out of the S&P500, and a new stock goes in. In this way, the S&P acts like a large, momentum-biased index.

INDU, aka the **DJIA**: Dow Jones Industrial Average, tracks the prices of 30 chosen big cap stocks. There are also indices for the Dow Utilities, and Dow Transportation stocks.

NASDAQ: The index tracking stocks trading on the NASDAQ stock exchange. It has a tech bias, and lower cap bias.

(Note: There are other indices, too, like the Russell 1000 and Russell 2000, but you don't need to learn about them here. If you can outperform the SPY over time, or at least the DIA, you're golden.)

Value Line: An information service that issues updated pages about public corporations, as well as ranking them by various criteria.

Compustat: Another information service that provides accounting and footnote information about public corporations, and enables CFAs and other analysts to screen for stocks with specific criteria.

Sleuth investing: Physical investigations of companies' non-accounting, non-categorizable attributes (on top of conventional stock analysis), used for obtaining a winning investment edge over those who don't do it.

If you liked this book,
look out for the author's next one:

HOW TO BUILD AN EMPIRE

(A Manual)

INDEX

www.ingramcontent.com/pod-product-compliance
Lightning Source LLC
Chambersburg PA
CBHW071159210326
41597CB00016B/1601
* 9 7 8 1 7 3 8 8 0 4 4 0 5 *